Asexuality

Asexuality Guide

Asexuality book about understanding the sexual orientation, tips, myths and misconceptions.

By

Corey Luckton

Table of Contents

Introduction

I want to thank you and congratulate you for buying this book. This book will help you to understand everything you need to know about asexuality. This will help you if you are an asexual person or if you know someone who is asexual.

Asexuality is one of the most misunderstood topics. There are some people who haven't even heard about it. There are many others who have heard the term, but dismiss its meaning because they believe that it has religious implications. There are many others who just refuse to accept the existence of asexuality and asexual people. These people go out of their way to make asexual people believe that they are not asexual after all.

Asexuality can be defined in simple words as a sexual orientation that is characterized by a definite lack of attraction towards any of the genders. Asexual people face many challenges. They need to acknowledge their asexuality without any guilt or shame. After they are able to accept it, they need to come out in front of people and let them know how they feel and function. It is important for people to understand that asexuality is a very normal sexual orientation. It would be so much easier for asexual people if other people took the trouble to understand what asexuality is. It is important not to speculate, but to understand a thing for what it is.

Most asexual people go through a phase of confusion and self-doubt. They will feel inadequate and will always have questions in their mind. If you are also battling through such a phase then you should know that this is very normal. There are many people out there who are going through such phases. All you need is the right information so that you can access and analyse for yourself. This book is an attempt to provide you with such information. This will help you to better understand your sexual orientation.

Being asexual is not a choice. You can't decide whether you wish to be asexual or not. You are either asexual or you are not. It is like other sexual orientations, where you have no say on how you feel. You need to know that sexual orientation will define and characterize your natural inclinations and attractions. However, it does not define or limit your actions. You are free to choose your actions, despite of your natural tendencies.

You need to know that asexuality is as normal as being a straight or a gay or bisexual. It is as simple as that. It is important that you educate yourself and break all the myths that surround the topic of asexuality. If you are asexual, it only means that you are different to most people and that some people may struggle to understand you, however this is purely due to lack of knowledge.

It is not an easy world for asexual people. The social setup makes it very difficult for the asexual to know of his/her asexuality. Sex is everywhere. You can find it on television, in movies, books, magazines and day to day conversations. This setup makes it very difficult for a person who doesn't feel sexual.

People believe in all kinds of myths and misconceptions about asexuality. They think that a person can suddenly turn into an asexual and come out of the phase, but it does not work that way. Asexual people just don't get a sudden awakening that they are asexual. It is a realization that comes when you make an attempt to understand your sexual orientation in a better light. It is seen that asexual people doubt their ability to function as normal human beings.

This book will help you to understand the very basics of asexuality. If you are an asexual, you will gain confidence in your sexual orientation. If you know someone who is an asexual, you can help the person to come out and accept their sexual orientation. This book will help you to appreciate and understand something that people have been avoiding for many years. It is important that asexuality is understood and appreciated as normally as any other sexual orientation. This book will try to address every question that you might have regarding asexuality. So, whether you are an asexual or not, this book will help you a great deal. It will educate you and make you more sensitive about things that deserve to be known.

Chapter 1. What Is Asexuality?

Sex actually motivates how people behave in their daily lives; many things that they do in their routine life are actually driven by their desire and need to have sex.

This might not be a very pleasant thought, but it is very much true. Sex is so much a part of our daily lives that people find it difficult to accept that for some people sex might not be a big deal.

Asexuality is a term that people don't understand. Even in today's Internet world where all the information is just a click away, people have very little knowledge about asexuality. The sad part is that sometimes even asexual people are not aware of asexuality. This is nothing but lack of knowledge and information.

There are many people out there who don't find sex exciting. They don't look at sex the way most people do. Sex isn't erotic for them. It is not pleasurable for them. They don't crave sex. It does not make sense to them in any way.

Would you call these different or abnormal? Do you also fall in this category of people? Or, do you know someone who does? Have you wondered whether this is some sort of abnormality or lack?

To begin with, you should know that a lack in sexual activities is not abnormal. It is as normal as having an interest in them.

For many people, asexuality is still a confusing term. They don't understand its meaning. This leads to a lot of confusion on this topic. If you make an attempt to clearly understand various sexual orientations, you will find it easier to define asexuality.

Asexuality can be defined in simple words as a sexual orientation that is characterized by a definite lack of attraction towards any of the genders.

Sexual orientation for a person is defined based on whom a person is sexually attracted to. Based on whether you are attracted to people of the same sex or opposite sex or both, your sexual orientation can be defined.

You are said to be heterosexual if members of the opposite gender attract you. On the other hand, you are said to be homosexual if members of the same gender attract you.

You will be bisexual if members of both genders, i.e. your gender and the opposite gender attract you.

If sexual orientation is defined by whether a person is attracted to the same gender, opposite gender or both genders, shouldn't it also include the scenario of not being attracted to any of the defined genders?

Asexuality bridges this gap. An asexual person does not feel sexually inclined towards another person.

Asexuality is by no means a disease. It does not mean that you are unwell or unhealthy. You should know that you have no medical condition whatsoever if you are an asexual person.

Asexuality is not based on any gender. You could be a man and be asexual. You could also be a woman and be asexual. Asexuality knows no country or religion. Asexual people don't look different or don't act weird, as some people might believe. They go about their life in a normal and simple manner like anyone else.

If you are wondering about what sexual attraction is then it is that strong attraction and sensation that you feel when you wish to see someone naked or when you wish to have sex with the person. It is that strong desire that you have when you wish to have sex. It is the arousal that you feel that might lead to sex. When you are sexually attracted to a person, you are attracted to a person in an erotic way.

An asexual person does not feel any such sexual attraction. In fact, the term sexual attraction can actually confuse an asexual because he/she has never felt it. Sexual attraction leads to a desire to have sex.

When an asexual person does not have sexual attraction, how can he/she have the same inclination, desire and understanding of sex as a non-asexual person? This is something that everybody needs to understand. The understanding of asexuality is rooted in this particular understanding.

What Isn't Asexuality?

While we are attempting to understand what asexuality is, it will also pay to understand what asexuality isn't.

Because people don't understand asexuality, they equate it with terms that sound similar. It is important to understand the differences between these terms. This will help you to know asexuality better.

- Asexuality does not mean that you are deficient in hormones such as testosterone or estrogen. An asexual has all the hormones that any other person would have.
- It does not mean that you are suffering from some disease and you need to get yourself treated for it. Asexuality does not define any medical disease.
- Asexuality does not mean that the person lacks sexuality. The person can indulge in sexual activities like any other person if he/she wishes to.
- It definitely does not mean that you are incapable of having sex. You might lack the natural drive to indulge in sexual activities, but you are very much capable of having sex like other people.
- If you are asexual, you are not straight; people of the opposite sex still fail to attract you in a sexual way.
- If you are asexual, you are also not a gay; people of the same sex fail to attract you in a sexual way.

- Asexuality definitely does not mean that you were abused or repressed in some way. It also does not define your religious preferences.
- Asexuality and virginity are different. This is a very important point. Just because you have not had sex does not make you an asexual person. This is explained in detail in the book.
- Asexuality is different from celibacy and abstinence. This is explained in detail in the book.
- Asexuality is not the same as fear of sex. Asexuality does not define any kind of fear. It is a sexual orientation, which has nothing to do with fear or love towards sex.

Is Asexuality A Choice?

There are many misconceptions surrounding asexuality. Many people fail to understand whether being asexual is a choice or not.

Being asexual is not a choice. You can decide whether you wish to be asexual or not. You are either asexual or you are not. It is as simple as that.

Can you decide whether you are heterosexual or gay? No, you can't because it is a natural tendency and not a personal choice. In the same manner, being asexual is your natural inclination and not your personal choice.

You can't decide one day that you will become asexual and give up sex. You can't decide that you will not get attracted to anyone from now on. It does not work that way.

If a person does not have sex for a few days, weeks, months or even years, does that mean that you are asexual now? No, having sex or not having sex is an action. It is your personal choice.

If you are unable to have sex because of reasons that are not personal, does that make you asexual? Irrespective of the reasons of not having sex, it is unrelated to a person's sexual orientation.

Asexuality only talks about the sexual attraction of a person. His or her sexual actions might be inspired from this tendency, but it will not have any effect on his or her asexuality.

Just because you decide that you want to become asexual, your natural tendencies will not die overnight. They will not vanish or change. Your choice will not be able to alter the way you naturally feel.

It is important to understand the difference between asexuality and celibacy. While you can decide to give up sex, you can't decide to not get attracted to other people. You can fight the attraction, but not negate it completely.

Sexual orientation does not define the behavior of a person

It should be clearly understood that the sexual orientation of a person does not define the behavior of the person. This section will help you to understand this.

Is it possible that a heterosexual man has sex with another man? A heterosexual man will naturally be inclined to have sex with a woman. However, this does not make him incapable of having sex with a man?

A heterosexual man can have sex with another man out of curiosity to know how it feels. It could just be an impulsive decision. The same is also true for a heterosexual woman. There is as much chance of her having sex with a woman as with a man.

There is a chance that a bisexual man is a virgin. He is attracted in a sexual way to both men and women. However, this does not rule out the probability that the man has never had sex ever.

Similarly, an asexual man or an asexual woman would be naturally inclined towards not having sex with either gender. However, this is no way rules out the probability that the asexual man or asexual woman has had sex.

You need to know that sexual orientation will define and characterize your natural inclinations and attractions, but it does not define or limit your actions. You are free to choose your actions, despite of your natural tendencies.

Sexual orientation does not define the emotional needs of a person

Your sexual orientation will define and characterize your sexual inclinations and attractions. It does not define or limit your emotional needs. Just because you are asexual does not mean that you will have limited emotional needs.

In spite of not getting sexually attracted to other people, asexuals are very much capable of forming intimate bonds. People should understand that sex and emotional ties are different.

They can be dependent on each other, but they can also exist without each other. An asexual person can be emotionally attached to other people.

Different people have different emotional tendencies. Some people are emotionally independent, while there are many others who are extremely emotionally dependent.

As an asexual person, you can fall into any of these categories. Your asexuality will not make you over emotional. It will also not make you a person who lacks any emotions whatsoever. A human being is bound to have emotions. You don't have to be afraid that your asexuality will kill your emotions. If your partner is an asexual, you can be sure that his or her emotional tendencies are not affected by the fact that he or she is asexual. This idea will be further explored later in this book.

It is a different topic that when asexuals are misunderstood, it will affect them emotionally. When you take away the right of a person to be true to his or her natural tendencies, he or she will be affected in every way possible, even emotionally.

What asexual people have to go through

Various studies and surveys have revealed that over one per cent of the population is asexual, but it is believed that the actual percentage would be more than one per cent.

Asexuals form the minority when we talk about various sexual orientations. However, just because something is in the minority does not mean that it is invalid. This is something that we all need to understand.

An asexual has to go through a lot in their daily routine life. Many a times, asexuals don't know that they are asexual. They believe what people make them believe. They are so pressured by the norms of society that anything against it is deemed as invalid. To break this circle, it is important that you understand it well. If you are an asexual, you should know how other asexuals feel. If you are not an asexual, you should know how your behavior can effect an asexual.

Family pressure:
Not everybody is lucky to get a progressive environment at home. Many people are still stuck in the age-old systems and beliefs. People did not understand asexuality in the past, and they don't attempt to understand it today. They think that it is a taboo and it should be completely avoided. They believe that if a family member is asexual, it is better to hide this fact to avoid embarrassment.

This regressive thought process in a family can make the life of an asexual very difficult. He or she finds it difficult to discuss confusions and thoughts with the family.

Societal pressure:
All of us have to face various kinds of pressure from society. There are certain rules and all of us have to abide by them, or be ridiculed.

We are expected to be a certain way. We are expected to talk and eat in a certain way. Things become worse for people who come from backwards areas and regions where people are still primitive in their thinking.

Many asexuals have been the victim of society pressures. They find it difficult to come out and share their feelings with people around them because of this pressure. They don't feel free and comfortable because they are different from the rest, and society doesn't accept that.

Being a laughing stock:

Asexual people become the laughing stock of their peer group. While some people might have an understanding and supportive group of friends, most people may not be that lucky.

As an asexual when you tell a group friends that you are not turned on by sex talks or that you are not interested in having sex, your friends might find that extremely hilarious.

Their attitude towards you will make you feel less of a human being. You might fall in the trap where you start doubting yourself.

Decreasing confidence:

Most asexuals go through a phase where they experience low self-esteem. This is a phase that they experience before they discover that they are asexual.

These people live in constant fear of not getting accepted by society. This feeling makes them feel inferior about themselves. They start believing that they feel different because they lack something.

Even after asexual discovers his or her asexuality, they have to deal with a lot of prejudices. If the asexual person is unable to cope with the pressure, they develop a gripping fear. While some asexuals are able to pull themselves out of this, others only go deeper down this road.

How would you feel if you are laughed at or made fun of? If someone makes fun of you once or twice, you can let that go. However, constant mockery can create havoc in a person's life. Such a person will see a decline in his or her confidence level. They may avoid talking to people to avoid being the butt of the joke.

The truth is that people are so ignorant that they assume that asexuality is some sort of disorder. They think that the asexual person is just trying to attract attention. They feel that they are in some way superior to them.

This sense of entitlement allows them to have fun at the expense of the asexual person, who has no choice but to slip into their shell.

Trying to look at sex like others:
Asexuality is one of our sexual orientations. If a person is asexual, he or she does not feel sexual attraction towards anybody. This very definition separates an asexual from the rest of the society.

While everyone around them looks at sex in a certain way, an asexual will always find their views different and will debate their ideas in their heads.

In a bid to be like others, the asexual might try to force themself to be like others. The asexual might go a step further and might even try to behave like people around them. They may pretend to like sex in order to get the approval of others.

This is what society does. The inability of our society to accept people the way they are makes these people so vulnerable and afraid of being themselves.

Chapter 2. Understanding Asexuality At A Deeper Level

We are always told that sex is an important part of a relationship. This conditioning makes it very difficult for us to accept that things can be different.

If you are trying to figure out whether you are asexual or not, it can be a real challenge. There is no denying this fact. You will have to understand the idea of asexuality in depth to know whether you are asexual or not.

As stated earlier in the book, asexuality is the absence of sexual attraction towards any of the genders in a person. This means that people who are asexual have the common trait of not being sexually inclined.

Though the definition of asexuality is simple and straightforward, it might not be enough for a person who is trying to understand their sexuality with the few limited experiences they have had.

Each asexual person will differ from another asexual person. This makes it all the more difficult. There can't be a list of ten points for you to checklist to ensure that you are an asexual person.

You have to understand your feelings and experiences and you have to learn from other people's experiences. This will also give you confidence and make you feel normal.

No one will ever come to you and tell you that you are asexual and you can be a part of the asexual club now. You have to educate yourself and understand your experiences in the best possible way.

Possible Scenarios Of Asexuality

If a person is asexual, they would have never felt the sexual attraction towards anybody, so how will they define its absence? How can you define the absence or lack of something that you have never had?

These questions can make things a little complicated if you are trying to figure out more about your sexual orientation. The definition of asexuality relies on negating a certain trait. If you have never experienced it, how do you negate it?

You should understand that there are no hard and fast rules. There are a few scenarios. You have to figure out which ones fit in your case. This will help you to better realize your orientation.

This book is designed in a way that you will be presented with different experiences and scenarios that can exist for you as an asexual person. It is not necessary that you experience all these scenarios.

Be open-minded and try to understand how asexuality can differ for each asexual person. This will help you to understand your sexual orientation.

A very tricky thing is that there is a possibility and probability that even if you identify with all the cases discussed in this section, you might not be an asexual.

The opposite is also very much true. There is also a possibility and probability that even if you identify with none of the cases discussed in this section, you might be asexual.

The point that is being made here is that there is no 100 per cent guaranteed result for determining sexual orientation. You have to understand your feelings and experiences and you have to learn from other people's experiences.

You can continue believing that you are a sexual person with a defect. This is the reason you don't enjoy sex. Or, you can gain knowledge about asexuality and accept that you are an asexual person.

The various experiences of various asexual people have helped us to design a few possible signs that can help you to determine whether you are asexual or not. The various possible signs are as follows:

You find sexual arousal unnecessary and distracting

As an asexual person, sexual arousal will be a waste of time for you. Most other people that you might know will have the urge to act on a sexual arousal. They will see it as a sign from the body that they need sex. But, for you it is just annoying.

You would rather have an arousal. You would rather just ignore any signal from your body because you work in a different manner. Your mind works in a different manner.

Even if you have an arousal, it is quite random. You are not fanaticizing about anybody or craving sex. The arousal is more a hindrance for you and you would rather not have such a thing.

You don't like masturbation

Most people masturbate because they can't get sex. As an asexual person, you have a different story. You will would masturbate than have sex, and in the most ideal scenario, you will not even masturbate.

You might have tried masturbation. There is a chance that you didn't like it. There is also the chance that you didn't understand its relevance in your life. You are fine even without it.

There is a strong probability that an asexual person hates masturbation. You might have tried it a couple of times, but you have come to realize that you dislike it and there is no reason for you to do it again.

There is also a possibility that as an asexual person, you do masturbate sometimes. But, masturbation for you is different for what it is for most other people. You just feel that it a bodily function and nothing else.

An asexual person will not have any guilt attached to the act of masturbation. It is not that they think that it is wrong if they masturbate. It is just that there is no real satisfaction that they feel when they masturbate.

You have never felt a strong attraction to another person

College is a place where young adults meet each other and get attracted to each other. This attraction is very much sexual and sometimes romantic. People have their first kiss and first kiss stories to boast about in college.

But, do you feel different? When your friend tells you about how they feel, do you feel confused? Do you find such talks alien? Do you feel that such interactions are complicated and unnecessary?

If you are asexual, you will always have a hard time believing people when they tell you their crushes and sexual attractions. It will always be difficult for you to understand what it is to feel this way.

You might never have had a crush. Even if you had one, you didn't feel about the person the way other people feel about their crushes. You never felt that having sex is an important part of a relationship.

A perfect relationship for you will have nothing to do with sex

For most asexual people, sex is nothing but a waste of time. Do you identify with this thought? Wouldn't you like to be close to a person who doesn't expect you to perform sexual activities?

Most other people that you might know will love sex, but for you it is only unnecessary and annoying. You will always have a hard time understanding the importance and real relevance of sex

You only have sex because your partner wants it

Asexual people can have romantic relationships with other asexual people and also non-asexual people. If you have been in a relationship, you would know that as an asexual, things were always different for you.

There are many asexuals who carry out sexual activities in a relationship with the partner only to satisfy the partner if they are non-asexual. This could be out of a feeling of guilt or responsibility for the partner.

We are always told that sex is an important part of a relationship. This conditioning makes it very difficult for us to accept that things can be different. Some people can do without sex and still be good in a relationship.

Do you feel that you are bisexual person who is not good at sex?

There is a high probability that you have also believed that you are a bisexual, but the only difference is that you are not good at sexual activities. You have believed that sex is not your thing.

This is a very common belief in many asexuals who have not yet discovered that they are asexual. They continue to believe that they are not good at sex, while the truth is that they lack sexual attraction towards anybody.

These people are not able to understand the difference between sexual attraction and the actual act of sex. Sex can be done even in the absence of sexual attraction.

These people also fall prey to many misconceptions that people around them could be carrying. They might start believing that they need to have more sex to finally get better at it.

No matter how much practice they do, they can't change their asexuality. They will end up feeling more miserable because they will always fall in a bracket that they still don't understand.

You have always believed that you have some kind of defect
You might have experimented a lot with various sex positions and different partners, but you might still be as confused as ever. A scenario like this makes an asexual believe that he or she has a defect or issue.

Many asexuals spend a major part of their adult life believing that they are lacking in some aspect. They believe that they are incompetent and lesser beings because of the defect that they have.

Some asexuals might get paranoid and might desperately look for ways to correct the defect. The truth is that it can't be corrected. The reason behind this is that there is no defect that needs to be corrected.

It is difficult for you to understand how a person can be hot
An asexual person will have a hard time relating to how a person can be hot. When your friend talks about his hot girlfriend, do you actually wonder as to what he even means. An asexual person has a hard term equating hot and sexy words with people.

An asexual person might see a person as attractive, charming, cute or pretty. They might equate words such as intelligent and smart with other people, but describing someone as hot and sexy is not their cup of tea.

Even if an asexual person tries to act cool in front of their friends and tries to be like them, they will always be troubled by an internal dialogue about such things. It should be noted that we are talking about how an asexual generally feels.

Some asexuals might fear ridicule from friends, and out of peer pressure, they might try to behave like everyone else is behaving. This is very much possible.

In spite of how an asexual person chooses to behave, he or she can't really ignore the way he or she is feeling. They will have to deal with the debate that is constantly going on inside them.

The exact scenarios might be different for all asexuals, but the base is quite the same. They all have to deal with some peer pressure along the way. They all have to deal with conflicting views in society.

If you go through all these things, then you could be an asexual. You will have to understand your confusions to come to a conclusion.

You are interested in sex in a non-sexual way
Although you generally do not feel the need to discuss sex at length, it does not repulse you. You find it interesting to see that another person doesn't see sex the way you do and that their body reacts to sexual stimulation differently.

You might look at sex in a way you look at mathematics and history. This is how sex interests you. For you, it will be how to study rather than how to participate in it. Most asexual people are comfortable reading about sex, how it works and which combinations work the best. They might even enjoy watching documentaries on them.

However, this is where their interest in sex would end. You would watch a documentary on the history of sex and forget about it. You will not have the uncontrollable urge to perform the act of sex.

Your friends will try to convince you that this is the only way to see it. You might even believe them. You might start to believe that you view sex in a wrong way.

You will try to keep your mouth shut the next time your friends discuss such sex scenes because you might feel that you are wrong in the way you look at sex. You might start believing that you are in a phase, and it will pass.

Asexuality is not a phase and it will not pass. Stop feeling ashamed of how you look at sex. You are the way you are. You were designed to be this way, and there is no right or wrong. Accept the way you look at things.

You will never get all the fuss that surrounds sex
Even if you are okay with the idea of sex, you will never see it in the light that others view it. You will always find it hard to believe that people are so mad for sex.

If someone comes to you and tells you that they haven't had sex for two weeks, you will not think it to be a great matter of concern. What is the big deal, anyway? While you still debate the idea of having sex or not, you find it very hard to believe that people actually chase it.

When you listen to the desperation of people looking for sex, you feel like you just need to get away. Such talks make you sick to the stomach because you don't understand them. How can someone be like that? What is the big deal?

The truth is that sex will never be a big deal for you. It does not imply that you are shy or uneducated. It definitely does not imply that you don't understand things. The thing is that sex is not the ultimate desire for you. It never was and it never will be.

As an asexual person, you will constantly be debating in your head in relation to what sex really means. An asexual person will always find it very difficult to come to terms with how most other people see sex.

All asexual people can go days and months without thinking about sex. They will always have a hard time understanding a person's fondness and dependence on sex.

You will always feel like a misfit in a group when they start talking about sexual endeavors and sexual jokes. You might laugh all those jokes, but the truth is that you will not understand these jokes most of the time.

Even if you like a person, the last thing you would want to do with them is sex. Sex means so little to you. The saddest thing will always be that people will never be able to understand this way of being.

Other people might encourage you to experiment a little more. They will tell you that you should be more excited and enthusiastic about sex because that is the only way to be.

Others might try to make you believe that there is something wrong with you. They might try to tell you that you lack in something that is so vital to the human existence. These thoughts will definitely confuse you.

Understand your experiences over the years

You need to understand all the experiences that you have had in the past few years. Understand them in the light of asexuality and see how they fit. This could be a real revelation for you.

It is better to accept and happily live with the fact that you are an asexual person, rather than believing all your life that there is something wrong with you.

Make a list of all the sexual experiences you have had over the years. Take a piece of paper and write everything. Write about what actually happened and how that made you feel. Try to track your emotions during those experiences.

The following sample experience list will help you to create one for yourself:

- I found the idea of my Cousin Mark's bachelor party very weird. What is a bachelor party supposed to mean? Everybody only had sex on their mind at that party. I have never felt so out of place.

- I never felt anything towards the supposedly hottest girl in the class. Yes, she was smart and intelligent. But, what was so sexual about this? Why would the boys gang up and discuss her for hours?

- I haven't had sex for two years, and I feel fine about it. Max didn't have sex for weeks, and he couldn't stop talking about it. What was so frustrating about not having sex for so long? Why would he discuss about it all the time?

- Why do people feel like sex is a triumph? Why do they boast about it all the time? Why don't I feel the same way?

- The time when my friends forced me to watch porn videos was a difficult one. I had no interest in what was going on. It was almost disgusting to watch it, but others were so excited. I couldn't say a word about how I felt because I thought something was definitely wrong with me.

- I faked all along with my girlfriend. I had no other way. She would be so excited about everything related to sex. I couldn't tell her how I feel because she'll only laugh at how incapable I am.

- I always try to keep quiet when people discuss sex. I don't know what else to do. I can't relate to their experiences. I fake a laugh most of the time. This is the best I do in such situations. I don't want them to think that I am incapable of having sex.

Chapter 3: Coming Out As An Asexual

When you decide to reveal your real identity to other people, you are actually coming out in front of those people. In regards to asexuality, coming out means letting people around you know that you are an asexual.

You should be well prepared when you decide to come out to your friends or family. You are sharing an honest part of yourself, so you should make all efforts to do it right.

If you speak to an asexual, you will realize that coming out has been an important part for them. It has made them feel more confident about themselves.

Because coming out is such an important part of your discovery and acceptance of the fact that you are an asexual, you should make sure that you do it in the best possible way.

The Relevance Of Coming Out

To begin with, you should understand the importance of coming out. There should be no need to do it if there is no real relevance attached to it.

When you decide to let people know your real self, you will feel relieved. There is no greater pleasure that being true to yourself.

This is like an answer to all the doubts that people had in their minds regarding you. This is also a chance to let your loved ones know why you feel the way you do.

When you reveal what you truly are, you are also in a way creating boundaries for people that they shouldn't cross.

Research well

It is important to know what you want others to understand. You can't expect your family and friends to understand you if you are not sure about stuff. You need to know about asexuality well if you are expecting others to understand.

You have to be sure that you are an asexual before you decide to break the news to everyone else. If you are not sure then it is better to take some time before you come out.

In this Internet age, it is all the easier to know about things. You should read about other asexuals and their experiences.

There are many bloggers that maintain regular blogs on the topic of asexuality. You should go through such blogs. Take your time because there is no hurry.

You will have unique experiences, but there would always be a common link. If you are an asexual, you will be able to understand the experiences of other asexuals. You will be able to find a common thread.

You should not assume that you are an asexual and just break the news to everybody. These topics are very sensitive and need to be handled with a lot of care.

If you read any blog on coming out for asexuals, the first step will always be to be sure that you are asexual. This is not to confuse you, but to make sure that you are not confusing asexuality with anything else.

Coming out to your parents and family

Family is the most important part of a person's life. If your family understands you and supports you, it becomes easier to deal with the rest of the world.

This makes it important to come out to your parents and the rest of the family. There is no harm in letting your parents know of your confusions and your revelations. This should only strengthen your bond and trust.

You know your parents the best. You would know how they see and understand the world. When you have decided that you should come out in front of your parents, you will have to look for the right opportunity to do so.

The tips discussed in this chapter will help you to plan the process in a better way so that there are no mistakes made.

Coming out to your friends and social circle

After your family, the next important structure in your life would be your friends and your social circle. Your social circle would comprise of your classmates in college or colleagues at work.

You will have to decide whether the people in your social circle deserve to know about your asexuality or not. It is not necessary to tell everybody about everything in your life.

While you may choose to let some of your good friends know about your truth, you might decide to skip many people. This is your choice and you know it best.

There should be no compulsion in this case. You should relax and race your brain through all the people that you know. You should decide which people need to know about your asexuality.

It is important that the people you come out in front of understand you and support. If you come out in front of the wrong people, they will pull you down.

Even if it is uncomfortable, you will have to share your asexuality with your partner. This is because the partner deserves to know about your reality.

Tips for asexual people to come out

As an asexual person, you will figure out the best way that works for you to come out in front of your friends and family. While each one will have his or her unique challenges, there are some tips that will help you to come out in front of other people.

The following tips and tricks have been shared for your benefit:

Be straightforward

There are several ways to say the same thing. You can beat about the bush. You can avoid a topic for days and months. But, the best way is to be as straightforward as possible.

It is important that you choose the right time and place to come out, but it is also important that you choose to be straightforward. Don't panic. Don't postpone the process. The sooner you can do it, the better it is for you.

If you expect people to understand you, you will have to make the effort to tell them exactly how it is that you feel. Talk to them about how you have been feeling. Tell them about how you discovered abut asexuality.

Don't be ashamed of yourself

If you are ashamed of yourself for something, what do you expect from others? Is asexuality something that you need to be ashamed of? Shouldn't people who refuse to acknowledge it be ashamed of themselves?

You should know that you have to be proud of your identity. You should be proud of yourself for making the effort to know more about asexuality. You should be proud that you accept yourself and refuse to be anyone else.

Whether you are homosexual, heterosexual, bisexual or asexual, you should be proud of yourself. There is no use staying in denial. Educate yourself and accept your sexuality. This will fill you with a confidence that you had never known before.

When you approach your friends and family to talk about your asexuality, fill your heart with pride and confidence. If you have guilt in the place of pride, you will only receive more of it. If you accept love and understanding, first learn to love yourself. Things will only get easier from there.

Don't look for acknowledgement

The more you look for other people's acknowledgement of you, the more disappointment you will face in your life. The more confident you are of yourself, the better your life will get.

If you come out with the wrong expectations, you will only be disappointed. You should never give anybody the chance to dismiss your identity. This will weaken your morale and will put you down as a person. This is the last thing that you should do to yourself.

No matter who you are coming out in front of, you should be sure that you are doing so because you wish the other person to know the real you. Don't wait for any acknowledgement or dismissal. Irrespective of what the other person feels, you should continue being proud of yourself.

When you are not looking for a specific outcome, it becomes easier to go through a process. When you know that you wish nothing from the other person, it will be easier to just share your feelings and experiences.

Approach a person you are most comfortable with

You might want to share your experiences with all your family members and friends, but you should start with the one you are most comfortable will. Even if the person is away from you, make an effort to connect with them.

If you talk to a person who understands you, it will get easier for you to share and open up. You will feel more confident and sure of what you wish to say. This will also allow you to avoid any nervousness and flipping out.

Avoid coming out in front of a group the very first time

The first time you decide to come out about your asexuality, you should try to avoid groups. You might have a big circle of friends, but keep the group small to open up to.

The reason behind this is that if there are more people, there is a chance that you will get nervous. If there is only one or two people, you will feel more confident and sure of what you wish to say.

If your first experience goes well, you will gain a lot of confidence. This will motivate you to come out in front of other people much more easily. The first experience is important because it will leave marks.

Be ready to deal with myths and misconceptions
An asexual person will have to deal with many myths along with their own insecurities. People will tell you all sorts of things. "You have a hormone problem", "You should take medication", etc.

Once you know that you are asexual, you should prepare yourself for all the misconceptions that people will throw at you. Read about all these misconceptions. This will allow you to be more informed.

It is important that no matter what people tell you, never fall for the myths. Believe in what you know is the truth.

Don't expect everyone to understand you
In your journey, you will find many people who will understand you and make efforts to make you feel comfortable, but this is not always the case.

If you come out in front of social circle, there is a chance a few people might not take it well. They will try to question you because they will believe that you are giving excuses to stay away from sex.

You will have to be prepared that some people will try to dismiss you and will render your feelings invalid.

Practice sessions
Practice makes perfect. This saying is true even when you are trying to come out. You should have many re-runs before you can approach your family and friends.

This will help you to gain the necessary confidence to approach people. You won't want to disappoint yourself by making a fool of yourself in front of people.

Test the waters

It is always better to test the water before you dive into it. This will inform you as to what you can expect and will also prepare you for the very best and the very worst.

The best-case scenario will be that your family and friends understand what you are trying to tell them and accept everything about your asexuality. The worst can be that people just dismiss you and your claims. They might even try to convince you against asexuality.

It is better to be prepared than to be sorry. You can be better prepared by knowing the views of your family and friends in advance. You should try to understand what they know of asexuality.

For example, if you are planning to come out in front of your parents, then before you actually do that, pick a day and time and talk to them about asexuality in a casual tone. Ask them what they know about it.

Try to assess their tone to know how they feel about it and how open they are to discuss about it. This will help you to prepare for your final coming out in a better way. If they are chilled out, you know you can easily talk to them. On the other hand, if they are closed towards the topic, you know that you will have to work harder to make them understand that it is not a big deal to be asexual. It won't alter your life in a negative way.

Chapter 4. Frequently Asked Questions

When it comes to asexuality, there are many assumptions that people make. They interpret it various ways, leading to a lot of confusion and doubt on this otherwise simple topic.

Even you might have several questions in your head regarding asexuals and asexuality. You might have wondered what kind of issues an asexual has to face.

Asking questions is a good thing. The more you ask, the more you understand. When you are attempting to understand asexuality, you should look for answers for even the silliest questions that you might have in your mind.

This chapter will attempt to address all the frequently asked questions surrounding asexuality. These questions and their answers will help you to understand asexuality in greater depth and will also help to clear all your misconceptions.

Does An Asexual Person Never Have Sex?

Asexual does not stand for the act of not having sex. To have sex or not to have sex is a choice and a decision that you make. You can decide to have sex even if you are asexual.

Asexuality will only define your sexual inclinations. You will not feel the need to have sex, but that does not mean that you can't have sex. You might not derive some real meaning or pleasure from it, but you can have sex like anyone else.

It should be clearly understood that an asexual person might have sex regularly. It is also possible that he or she does not have sex at all. It is also possible that he or she has never had sex. There is also a possibility that he or she has it sometimes.

So, basically anything out of the given scenarios is possible. However, what remains constant is that the asexual person will not experience sexual attraction, which mostly motivates people to have sex.

Can You Cure Asexuality?

This is a classic question that many people ponder. It has been a great matter of concern whether asexuality can be cured or not. Parents are worried if they know their child is asexual.

They wish and wonder if they can cure this condition of the child. People wish to cure it because they think that asexuality is a hindrance and a problem.

They believe that asexuals are incapable of leading normal and happy lives. They think that if someone is an asexual, they are not normal. They believe that the only way to help an asexual is to cure their asexuality.

Diseases and disorders can be detected and cured, but you can't cure something that is perfectly normal. You have to understand that asexuality is a very normal thing.

You can't cure asexuality because it is not a disease. It is a natural tendency of a person. This natural tendency is not abnormal so it can't be cured.

People have a tendency to fear things that they don't understand. Just because they don't understand the true meaning of asexuality, they start believing that is an abnormal condition. This helps them to hide their ignorance.

You should try to gain knowledge about things that you don't understand. Just because you don't know something does not mean that it is not real or normal. Your normal could be different to other people's normal.

How Can You Know If A Person Is Asexual?

There is no bulb that will light up when you are near an asexual person. You can't look at a person and judge that he or she might be asexual.

Just because a person walks a certain way, talks a certain way, eats a certain way or dresses in a certain fashion does not mean that the person is asexual. You can't guess such things about another person.

There are no physical indicators of an asexual person. Even if the person is naked in front of you, there is no way to tell whether he or she is asexual or not.

If you are expecting that you will be able to know whether a person is asexual or not by closely observing how they behave, you will fail to do so. The person will be as normal as any other person.

The only way of knowing whether the other person is asexual or not is by asking them. There are no indicators that will help you to decide just by glancing at a person that is asexual.

How Can A Person Become Asexual?

There is no switch in your body that you can turn on to become asexual. It does not work that way. You can't decide whether you wish to be asexual or not. You are either asexual or you are not. It is as simple as that.

You can't decide that you will become asexual. You can't decide to not get attracted to other people. So, if you are planning on becoming asexual, then you are in for a disappointment. There is no such thing as becoming an asexual. Your sexual orientation is not your choice.

You can control it and force yourself to behave in a certain way, but there is no way to change it. For example, if you are an asexual, you have the choice of still having sex every day. And, if you are non-asexual, you can still give up sex.

Is Asexuality Gender Dependent?

No, it is not gender dependent. No kind of sexual orientation is dependent on the sex of the person. A heterosexual person can be either a man or a woman. A homosexual person can be either a man or a woman; the same goes for all sexualities. Similarly, an asexual person can be either a man or a woman.

This might look very obvious to some people, but often simple queries and confusions like these can lead to bigger misconceptions.

Can An Asexual Man Have An Erection?

An asexual man can have an erection. Asexuality is in no way a physical condition. A man that can't have an erection has a physical issue. Asexuality and the ability to have erections are unrelated.

If you talk to an asexual man, he will tell you can his asexuality does not affect his penis erection. It is just like any other man would have it. A man who can't have an erection is said to have an erectile dysfunction.

Can An Asexual Person Fall In Love With Someone?

This is another question that haunts many people. They feel that asexual people are incapable of falling in love. This is nothing but a myth. Many asexuals around the world have been and are in love.

The sexual orientation of a person is not a means to judge whether they can sustain love or not. Asexual people can get into romantic relationships just like most other people. Yes, the dynamics of the relationship will be different. The asexual person would not have the urge to pounce on their partner every hour of the day, but the lack of sexual attraction does not make them incapable of love. They can love anyone else and they also deserve to be loved like anyone else. Love is more an emotion that is attached to human nature and less to sexual needs and wants.

Can An Asexual Person Have Kids?

Asexuality and fertility are two separate topics. If you are a fertile man or a fertile woman, you can make the decision to have kids with your partner. This is a personal choice that you can make.

Just because you are asexual does not mean that you are not capable of being a mother or a father. There are many sexually active people who can be infertile. Sexual inclinations and fertility are two separate things. It is better to understand this.

Many asexuals around the world are happy mothers and fathers. The asexual person has all the right hormones and genitals. He or she has everything that is required of him or her to be a mother or father biologically.

Chapter 5. Myths and misconceptions

When people don't understand something, this leads to a lot of confusion in their minds, thus leading to myths and misconceptions.

People don't realize that the misconceptions that float around can be offensive and also hurtful. If you don't understand something, you should try to gain knowledge rather than mocking it.

It is often seen that asexuals become the butt of many hurtful jokes. Such an attitude only puts them down. You might forget about it, but the person could be damaged in a very severe way.

The biggest problem is that often asexuals are so caught up in various misconceptions, that they start focusing on the wrong things. They start feeling that there is something seriously wrong either with them or the world.

Asexuality Does Not Exist

Even after all the books, blogs and movements that are dedicated to asexuality, some people don't want to believe that asexuality is a reality. These people try to shun anyone who tries to talk to them about asexuality.

These people firmly believe that people who talk about asexuality or who claim to be asexual are just wannabes that wish to attract some attention towards them.

This is a crazy myth. Asexuality definitely does exist, otherwise this book wouldn't exist. People who still wish to believe that asexuality does not exist want to live in a bubble where everything they know is the truth and everything they fail to understand is false. Asexuality deserves the respect and acceptance the same as any other sexual orientation.

Asexuality Is A Phase… If You Wait, You'll Grow Out Of It

You might have heard this many times. If you share your asexuality with someone, they will conveniently tell you that this is a phase. Like all temporary phases, this will also pass.

They will tell you different ways to get past this phase. "You should pray if you don't already do it." "You should meditate more." "You should think about better things in life."

Ignorant people will try to convince an asexual that he or she is going through a phase. There is a lot of difference between a phase and an orientation.

A phase is a short spell that will eventually go away. An orientation is no spell that will pass away with time. An orientation is a natural characteristic that you are born with and that you will live with.

You Should Get Laid, That Will Cure Your Asexuality

This is another misconception in the minds of many people. They believe that an asexual person feels that way because they have never had sex or not had sex in a long time, or even if they had, it wasn't with the right person.

They believe that if they find someone better to have sex with, they will get out of this asexuality. They might tell you have sex 'x' number of times before deciding that you are not sexually attracted to anyone.

It is funny that people believe that sex is the real cure for asexuality. How can this be possible? It is like saying that if you don't have the urge to eat pizza, then eating lots of pizza will cure your problem.

The truth is that no matter how many times you have sex, you can't change your sexual orientation. It will be what it has always been. You can't decide that you will not get attracted to anyone from now onwards.

An Asexual Person Is Actually Gay

For many people, asexuality is still a confusing term. They don't understand its meaning. This leads to a lot of confusion on this topic and they tend to believe that asexual is a fancy term for gay.

However, this is definitely not true because gay and asexual are two different sexual orientations. You can't replace one with the other.

Sexual orientation for a person is defined based on whom a person is attracted to. Based on whether you are attracted to people of the same sex or opposite sex or both, your orientation can be defined.

Asexuality can be addressed as a sexual orientation that is defined by a definite lack of attraction towards any of the genders. On the other hand, you are said to be homosexual or gay if members of the same gender attract you in a sexual way.

Being asexual is your natural inclination and not your personal choice. If you make an attempt to clearly understand various sexual orientations, you will find it easier to define asexuality.

Maybe You Haven't Met The Right Person

This is also a misconception in the minds of many people. They believe that an asexual person has been hanging out with the wrong people… "If he finds someone better, he will get out of this asexuality".

Sometimes, many asexuals also start believing in this myth. An asexual person might start frantically hooking up with people just to meet that right person. This will lead to a lot of frustration in the person.

They might start feeling that there is something seriously wrong either with them or the world; otherwise they would have found the one they would have felt the sexual attraction towards, surely?

The truth is that no matter how many right people you meet in your life, you can't change your sexual orientation. It will always be the same..

Asexuals Need A Better Partner

This myth is similar to the last one. People believe that with the right partner, asexual people can work on their asexuality.

The truth is that there is no need to work on the asexuality of a person. What is required is that people let other people be. It should not be so difficult to accept people of other sexual orientations.

Why it is even expected that asexuals treat themselves? What is there to treat? They are a little different from you. But does that stop you from accepting the truth that they are as normal as you?

Asexuality Is A Religious Term

The truth is that asexuality does not adhere to any religious or spiritual propaganda. Asexuals are not trying to spread anything. They are trying to live peacefully like everybody else. They are not trying to convert or recruit anyone.

By believing in myths like these, people make it all the more difficult for the sexual minorities. They need to be respected for what they are, rather than being accused of something that they have nothing to do with.

Asexuals Are Just People Recovering From A Past Traumatic Experience

Some people like to believe that an asexual person is someone who has had a traumatic experience in the past, something like sexual abuse. This trauma forces them to get averse to sex and sex talks.

This is again nothing but a myth. A past traumatic experience has nothing to do with the sexual orientation of a person. What will you call those people who have had such experiences and still enjoy sex?

Asexuals don't hate sex. There is no back-story. They are orientated in a different way, that is it. They just don't feel sexually attracted.

Asexuality Is For People Who Have An Identity Crisis

The truth is that anyone can have an identity crisis. Asexuality has nothing to do with identity crises. Just because you see a person confused, lifeless and lost, you can't call them asexual. They could be battling some emotional trauma or professional problem.

The very fact that people misunderstand asexuality and asexual people leads to an environment where asexuals feel low and inadequate. If people were more understanding, asexuals wouldn't have to go through what they go through.

People Who Fail At Dating Start Calling Themselves Asexual

This one is another classic myth that some people believe in. It is hard to debate with people who believe in such myths, but the fact is that this is an absolute lie.

Asexual people may or may not date. It depends on them. Anyone can fail in dating; heterosexual, homosexual, bisexual or asexual. Success or failure in dating different people will have no effect on your sexual orientation.

People Who Are Unattractive Become Asexual

There are some people who firmly believe that people who talk about asexuality or who claim to be asexuals are just unattractive people who wish to attract some attention.

This is one of the worst myths that asexuals have to deal with. This is a way of putting someone down. We need to appreciate everyone because everybody is attractive in their own way.

Sexual orientation has nothing to do with how a person looks, and asexuals are not trying to gain attention in any way. They are looking for acceptance and nothing more than that.

Asexuality Is Contagious

Diseases are contagious. How can something that is not a disease be contagious? Asexuality is not a disease. There is no chance that it can be contagious. Sexual orientation can't be transferred or passed on.

Just because you hang out with an asexual person does not mean that you will also become asexual. Your sexual orientation will remain what it is irrespective of whether you choose to hang out with asexuals or not.

Asexuals Are A Group Of Rejected People

Some people also believe that all the losers of the world have formed a group called the asexuals. These people raise slogans and crib and cry so that they can garner some attention in their otherwise boring lives.

This myth is another product of lack of knowledge. When people don't understand things, they start putting labels on it. It is better to admit that you don't know anything about asexuality than to put such labels on asexuals.

Asexual People Are Boring

This will entirely depend on what a person thinks is interesting. To a person who only wants to do sex or talk about sex, an asexual person can seem to be very boring.

Asexual people are normal people. They do everything that other normal people do. You can go out and have fun with your asexual friend without any problem whatsoever.

People are very different from each other. While some like painting, others like hiking. While some enjoy cooking, others do not. You will find a person interesting if they enjoy the same activities as you.

If your asexual friend enjoys the same activities as you do, he would be interesting to you. On the contrary, if he doesn't enjoy those things, you'll find him boring. However, in either case, his asexuality has no role to play in it.

Asexuality Is Evolution's Population Control

A person who understands asexuality even in the most basic way will know that this is a myth. An asexual person can contribute towards increasing the population just like non-asexuals.

Asexuality is no way to control the population. An asexual is capable of having sex and having kids, as has been explained earlier.

Asexuality Is Another Way To Define The Morality Of A Person

There are some people who believe that asexual people think that they are asexual because they have high morality. These people think that asexuals are people who don't believe in having sex before marriage.

This is nothing but a misconception. The morality of a person and the sexual orientation of a person are completely unrelated.

Chapter 6. Masturbation and Asexuality

There is a lot of confusion in the minds of people relating to the presence or absence of masturbation in an asexual person's life. Though masturbation is a personal topic people are not comfortable discussing, you need to understand it in relation to asexuality.

Do asexual people masturbate? What do they need masturbation for? Isn't masturbation a sexual activity? Shouldn't asexual people stay away from it?

There are so many questions that an asexual person is hounded with. It is important that all these questions are addressed, so that all the confusion from the minds of people can be eradicated.

Some people think that asexuals must have an aversion towards masturbation. They believe that masturbation can hamper a person's asexuality. If a person masturbates, does he or she lose his or her asexuality?

There are so many points that need to be addressed in relation to masturbation. This chapter is an attempt to view masturbation from the point of view of an asexual.

Various scenarios are discussed in this chapter. There are no fixed rules. As an asexual, you will be able to relate to some or all of these scenarios.

Do Asexual People Masturbate?

Asexual people can masturbate. It is not a rule that they do and it is also not a rule that they don't. There are many asexual people who masturbate, while there are many others that do not masturbate.

It is important to understand here that masturbation is the choice of the person. If the asexual person wishes to masturbate, they can. It will not take away from the fact that they are asexual.

It is more like a bodily function for them. It has nothing to do with them being sexually attracted. Masturbation is not categorized into asexual masturbation, homosexual masturbation or heterosexual masturbation.

Masturbation is simply masturbation. A heterosexual has the choice to masturbate or not. A homosexual also has the choice to masturbate or not. Similarly, an asexual person has the choice to masturbate or not.

It is also important to understand here that masturbation is an act that is done with the help of sexual organs. It is a sexual response of the body. This makes it all the more clear that asexual people can experience sexual pleasure.

There is a myth that asexuals can't experience anything sexual in their body. People like to believe that asexuality is a mask to cover the non-functioning sexual organs of a person. This is nothing but false. The very fact that asexuals can masturbate is a simple way of explaining that asexuals have all the sexual organs working for them. Sexual orientation is not defined by such factors.

An asexual person can have similar sexual responses of the body as a sexual person. They can have similar sexual properties and can experience sexual pleasure also. You might be surprised to know that many asexual people also find it hard to believe that they can experience sexual responses of the body and still be asexual. Confusion regarding the same creates havoc in an asexual person's mind.

Imagine that you find traits of asexuality in you and also enjoy masturbation. This scenario can confuse even an asexual person. You should know that asexuality defines only your attraction quotient. It does not define or limit your actions. As an asexual person, you will experience a lack of attraction to any of the sexes, but you can still masturbate or even have sex.

Asexuality is the measure of the sexual orientation of the body. It is not the measure of the behavior of a person. Masturbation is the behavior that you choose. It has nothing to do with orientation.

It should also be noted here that asexual men and women can both masturbate. It is not that only asexual men can experience the pleasures of masturbation.

Many asexual women are known to masturbate. They derive pleasure from it and are also able to relieve stress and tension from the body.

The Need For Masturbation For An Asexual Person

Once it is established that an asexual person can masturbate, the next obvious question is as to why they need to masturbate. What could an asexual gain from masturbation?

An answer to this question will also help you to understand the importance of masturbation. Masturbation is often linked to the act of deriving pleasure from the genitals in absence of another person to perform sex.

While the above definition is true, this isn't the only purpose of masturbation. Not everybody masturbates because sex is unavailable. It is important to understand masturbation with a broader perspective.

It is also important to understand the importance of masturbation in an asexual person's life. If an asexual person does not have sexual desires, what does he or she need masturbation for? What purpose does masturbation hold for an asexual person?

The following points will help you to understand the importance and significance of masturbation in an asexual person's life:

- **Relaxation**: The person might need to relieve stress in their body. This stress is not caused by any sexual deprivation. In fact, the person could be feeling stress because of any reason.

Masturbation can be a tool to relax and feel better by relieving stress.

- **To get rid of boredom**: This could come as a surprise to many, but this is one of the reasons of an asexual to masturbate. An asexual person is as normal as any other person. He or she could indulge in masturbation to avoid boredom. There is nothing sexual about this. Just like a person watches movies or listens to songs to get rid of boredom, they might masturbate.

- **To avoid embarrassing situations**: It has been stated earlier that the asexual person is as much capable of having sex as any sexual person. The genitals of an asexual person can embarrass them sometimes. Men can get an erection and nocturnal secretions. To avoid any such embarrassing situation in front of other people, the person might decide to masturbate in spite of the lack of sexual desire to do so. It is more like a task to them that needs to be done.

- **To reduce period pain**: It is believed that masturbation can help a woman to feel better during her period, as masturbation can significantly reduce period pain. An asexual woman might decide to masturbate because of this reason. Many asexual women are known to masturbate regularly because this helps them to feel better when they are on their period.

- **Bodily function**: Masturbation is like a bodily function for them. It has nothing to do with them being sexually attracted. The mind of an asexual person will always work in a different way. While a sexual person will focus on sex, the asexual mind will work in a very different way.
- **Experimentation**: An asexual person can be curious by nature. They can have the itch to know more about their body

or have the desire to know whether their sexual organs are working fine or not. This simple itch can motivate them to experiment. An asexual person can indulge in the act of masturbation just for some fun and for experimentation purposes.

- **Health reasons**: There are health-related reasons that can motivate a person to masturbate. For example, men can masturbate because they wish to make sure that their prostate is healthy and there is no impending health issue related to it. This is a very technical reason to perform masturbation, and many well-informed asexual people are known to masturbate because of such technical reasons.

- **To enjoy orgasms**: There should be no shame for an asexual person to admit that even they can enjoy orgasms. This does not change their sexual orientation. Again, it depends on the person. Some asexual people will enjoy orgasms, while there will be others who will not find any pleasure in orgasms.

- **No specific reason**: Having no specific reason to masturbate is also a good enough reason to masturbate. It is quite possible that the asexual person has no reason whatsoever to masturbate other than because they feel like it.

It is sincerely hoped that the above points are able to make you understand the various reasons behind masturbation. These reasons can be simple but are very relevant. This understanding will help you to understand asexuality better.

Fantasies for an asexual person

You might be wondering whether an asexual person fantasizes or not while masturbating. This is a doubt that is very natural if you are trying to understand the concept of asexuality in great detail.

Just like the act of masturbation, fantasizing is also a very personal thing. There are many asexual people who fantasize when they masturbate, while there are many others that do not fantasize.

It is important to understand here that this is the choice of the person. It is more like what works for a person. What works for you might not work for me.

If the asexual person wishes to fantasize, they can. It will not take away from the fact that they are asexual in their sexual orientation.

Similarly, if the asexual person wishes not to fantasize while they masturbate, they can do so too. Even this act will not take away from the fact that they are asexual.

This concept can be very difficult for many people to understand. If the person can fantasize a sexual activity, doesn't this mean that they are sexual in their nature and orientation? No, it does not mean so.

For asexual people who fantasize during the act of masturbation, it is more like fantasizing a faceless person in a certain position to aid their masturbation. There is no sexual inclination towards a person or gender.

It is more like a bodily function for them. If the act of fantasizing makes the process of masturbation easier then why not do it? It has nothing to do with them being sexually attracted.

Having said that it is also important to note that there are many people who are asexual and they indulge in masturbation without any fantasizing involved whatsoever. This is also perfectly fine.

We have reached the end of this chapter and by now, you should be able to appreciate a simple fact that there are many asexual people who masturbate, and there are many others who don't masturbate.

Within this framework, it is further possible that the asexual person fantasizes when he or she masturbates, but it is also possible they some don't.

If you are asexual and still figuring out the various aspects of your asexuality, then you should understand that it is perfectly normal to fall into any of these categories. It will not take away from your asexuality in any way.

You can try to masturbate, see if that works for you. It is fine either way. If you like masturbation, you should try fantasizing. See if that works for you. Again, it is fine either way.

Chapter 7. Sex and Asexuality

Do asexual people have sex? What do they need sex for? How does sex satisfy ?hem Isn't sex a sexual activity? Shouldn't asexual people stay away from sex? Isn't sex wrong for them? The confusion surrounding sex and asexuality has led to such questions. Because of the way the word 'asexuality' sounds, people like to believe that it is limited to sex.

If a person can enjoy sex then they definitely can't be an asexual, right? There are many asexuals who believe in such myths until they discover what it is really to be an asexual. The truth is far from what people believe. Asexual people can have sex. It is not a rule that they do and it is also not a rule that they don't. There are many asexual people who have sex, while there are many others that do not have sex.

It is important to understand here that sex is the choice of the person. Similarly, if the asexual person wishes not to have sex, they can do so too. Even this act will not take away from the fact that he or she is asexual in their sexual orientation. Sexual orientation and attractions are different to the act of sex.

It is more like a bodily function for them and it has nothing to do with them being sexually attracted. Sex is not categorized into asexual sex, homosexual sex or heterosexual sex. Even if an asexual decides to have sex on a regular basis, it is never erotic for them.

This chapter will help you to understand sex from the point of view of an asexual. You will be able to understand sex from a different perspective.

Understanding Sex

It is very important to understand sex from the point of view of an asexual person. There are many people who assume that an asexual stands for everything anti-sex. They believe that an asexual has nothing to do with matters of sex.

This is not true. When you dig deeper in the matters of asexuality, you will understand that sex is much more than what we perceive it to be.

If you are asexual but can't find a connection between your sexual endeavors and your sexuality, wouldn't that create havoc in your life? As an individual, you will deteriorate each day if you don't understand where you belong.

Asexuality is a simple way to define the sexual orientation of the body. It is not a measure of the behavior of the person. Sex is a choice of behavior and it has nothing to do with orientation.

Sex is not just an answer to the body's sexual needs. It is also connected to the ego of a person. There are so many reasons to have sex apart from sexual attraction towards another person.

It is very important that you clearly understand that asexuality defines only your attraction quotient. It defines your sexual attractions. You can have sex even if you are not sexually attracted to a person.

Shouldn't Asexual People Be Virgins?

An asexual person may or may not be a virgin. There are many asexual people who have never experienced sex and there are many others who have done it a few times. Then there are other asexual people who are in sexual relationships and have sex on a regular basis.

An asexual person can also have multiple partners and multiple sexual relationships. This is more a question of their views than a question on his asexuality. If you are a virgin, it doesn't imply that you are an asexual. You could be a heterosexual, homosexual, bisexual or asexual. It could be related to your moral values, also. It could be because you never got the chance to get intimate with someone. These all are possibilities. There is no specific rule in this regard.

How Can An Asexual Person Have Sex?

This is a question that never leaves an asexual person. All those people who are trying to understand their sexuality should understand these topics with precision. This will help them to feel more confident and better about themselves.

Have you never heard of a heterosexual man who had sex with a woman or man he was not necessarily sexually attracted to? It can happen with a person of any sexuality and not just asexual people.

As an asexual person, you will experience a lack of attraction to any of the sexes, but you can still have sex. The opposite is also true. You can choose not to have sex. There is nothing that you will lose if you decide so.

There are many asexual people who find it hard to believe that they can experience sexual responses of the body and still be asexual. It is important to clear such doubts and confusions as early as possible.

How would you define sex? Sex is an act that is done with the help of an individual's sexual organs. It is a sexual response of the body, which is performed with another person.

Sex is an act that you can choose to perform or not. You will also have the choice irrespective of your sexuality. You can refrain from sex even if you are sexually attracted to others. The opposite is also very much true.

Having sex or not having sex will not take away from the asexuality of a person. You might take some time to take to this concept, but if you experience no sexual attraction and yet indulge in sex, you should know that this is fine. Nothing is wrong with you.

Sex is just an act. A heterosexual has the choice to indulge in it or not. A homosexual also has a similar choice. So, why shouldn't the same apply to an asexual person? An asexual person also has the choice to have sex or not.

An asexual person does not have a defect of any sorts in their sexual organs. These organs produce the same hormones like the organs of homosexual and heterosexual people. So, an asexual person can also use these sexual organs.

Asexual people can experience sexual pleasure. There is nothing right or wrong in this, it is just the way it is. An asexual person can have similar sexual responses of the body as a sexual person.

Can An Asexual Person Only Have Sex With Asexual People?

An asexual person can have sex with an asexual person and also a non-asexual person. There is no rule that an asexual should only have sexual encounters with other asexuals.

When you meet a person, like them and decide to get physical, do you know the sexual orientation of the person? How can you possibly know that? As a heterosexual person, how would you know that the other person is not asexual or bisexual?

The truth is that there is no way of determining this. If the person chooses to share their sexual orientation with you, it is only then that you will know. An asexual person can have sex with you normally like any other person.

This eliminates the idea that an asexual person can have sex with only an asexual person. An asexual person can have sex with an interested asexual person or an interested non-asexual person. The point is that both the people need to be interested in sex, irrespective of their sexual orientations.

Sex From The Point Of View Of An Asexual Person

An asexual person will view sex in a very analytical way. They might even get bored in middle of the act. It is a different question whether they choose to voice their opinion or not.

Most asexual people will only be remembering what they are supposed to be doing. They would be wondering if they are doing it right. Am I too fast? Shouldn't I kiss now? What should I do next? The person might feel a sense of disconnect throughout the act.

Sex is often spoken about in the most pompous way. Even before we have experienced it, we are made to believe that it is the best thing that can happen to mankind. Most of us get into it with such a perception.

Each individual will have their own understanding of sex, but most asexual people will feel nothing great about it. They will question all the earlier beliefs that they had about how great sex would be.

As an asexual person, you might often debate in your head why people have sex if this is what it is? While most people you know will have their fondest memories of sex, you will only have confusion.

You should also understand that every asexual person will have their own personal experiences. Each one will have a different tale to tell. While we can give general conclusions, the specifics will always be different.

There might be many asexual people who might feel an emotional connection and a sense of warmth if they perform sex with someone they are in love with. They might even prefer sex over masturbation.

Asexual people can also enjoy the physical part of sex, but it is always more technical for them. They will always be more interested in understanding why a certain thing can work and why another can't.

Some asexual people might enjoy sex because they might find it different and interesting, and they would want to explore it more. However, it would not be the best thing that they have experienced. It will just be a good and different experience.

It is not surprising for an asexual person to question the importance of sex in the world. They will always find it hard to believe that people can destroy each other and kill each other for sex. What is so great about it?

Things To Know If You Are In A Sexual Relationship With An Asexual Person

There are no physical limitations in an asexual person when it comes to sex. If there are any physical limitations, then that is related to the individual's sexual capabilities. It has nothing to do with the asexuality of the person.

Another point that needs to be addressed here is that in spite of not having physical limitations regarding to sex, a person can still not have sex. There could be other factors that could be behind this.

There are many asexual people who may refrain from sexual activities because they wish to or because they are not in a kind of relationship where they feel that they need more closeness physically and emotionally.

It might just not be the right time for the asexual person to indulge in sex. Even if your asexual partner has sex with you, you will feel that their desire to have it is different from yours, if you are non-asexual. They will not crave it the way you would.

You should never pressure an asexual person to have sex. If you think that taking them on a guilt trip and forcing them to have sex is the right way, then you are highly mistaken.

Your asexual partner is not trying to trouble you by being difficult. It is just the way it is for them. In the same way that you can't understand their lack of interest for sex, they can't understand your need for it.

Communication is the only key when there is a sexual relationship between an asexual and a non-sexual person. You will have to come to a common ground if you wish this to work for the two of you.

It is important that the commitment and the compromise are respected from both sides. Discuss how you feel and what you want. Let the other person also discuss the same with you.

Don't be harsh and hard on one another. Talk to each other and make an attempt to understand how the other functions. In addition, accept that they are very different from what you are as an individual.

For you, sex might be the union of two souls, but maybe your asexual partner feels nothing like this. You have to accept that while you might be mad after your sexual partner, your partner might not be sexually attracted to you. It has nothing to do with you.

Don't put yourself down because you see the lack of sexual lust. As partners, you need to be compassionate towards each other. You should respect each other for things better than sex. It is important that you understand that your partner comes from a different place than you.

Another thing that you should know when in a relationship with an asexual person is that you will find that the individual will slowly withdraw from sex. The frequency will reduce with time.

This again has nothing to do with you. While you might think that they don't love you anymore, the truth could be something else.

In the beginning of the relationship, the asexual partner might feel guilty that they can't satisfy you sexually. They might take this as a challenge and might try to prove a point.

But no matter how hard they try, they can't change this basic nature. They will slowly start getting bored. You will see them avoiding sex as much as possible. This can be a very tricky situation for you and your partner.

The key again is communication. You have to address your concerns with your partner. You can create a better world for yourself and your partner by being more open and kind towards each other.

Shouldn't All Asexual People Feel The Same About Sex?

This is a misconception in the minds of many that all asexual people should feel the same about sex. They all should hate it and never want it. This is definitely not true.

There are various opinions that different asexual people can have. Some might not care much, some might enjoy it and some others might just hate it.

Asexuality will only mean that the person feels no sexual attraction. His or her thoughts and actions beyond this point are very personal and individual. All of them don't have to feel the same way.

It should be noted that the thinking of a person is affected by various factors, such as upbringing, experiences and education. An asexual in the suburbs of Bombay will think differently from an asexual studying in New York. The sexual orientation of a person will also affect his or her thoughts about sex, but in the long run it is much more than that. So, if you are expecting that all asexuals will sit in a line and raise slogans against sex, then this is not going to happen.

Chapter 8.   Attraction, Love And Marriage In Asexuals

People assume that asexual people have no feelings whatsoever. They like to believe that asexuality means a defect in your ability to feel love and to give love. But, this is nothing but false.

Asexuality does not restrict a person from falling in love or even from getting married. You need to understand what love is and what marriage is. This will help you to understand the point that is being made here.

This chapter will help you to address all the questions pertaining to asexuality, love and marriage. All the 'hows' and 'whens' will be attempted to be answered in this chapter.

Do Asexual People Want To Be Alone?
No, this is nothing but untrue. People assume that asexuality means that the person is making accuses to stay alone. They assume that they want to be alone.

If a person wishes to be alone, it is his or her individual choice. Even a bisexual or gay person can wish to be alone. This has more to do with their individual lives and their experiences.

Asexual people can look for company just like any other person. They will invest in good relationships and friendships.

Isn't Love And Sex The Same?
Many people might want to believe that sex and love are the same, but they are not. A person can be in love with another person's nature, personality and identity, and yet not get the desire to have sex with them.

While most people want to have sex with the beautiful girl they are in a relationship with, the asexual person will appreciate the beauty of the girl, be in love with her and still not want to have sex with her.

Love is much more than the act of sex. This chapter is an attempt to understand all the forces that come to play when you are falling in love with the other person.

While most people like to believe that it is only sexual attraction that leads to love, this is not true. There is romantic attraction and aesthetic attraction that are equally important. You will learn about these types of attractions shortly.

Asexuality And Marriage

Asexual people also get married. This is not a miracle. In fact, this is as normal as a bisexual marriage. Why shouldn't an asexual get married?

People have all kinds of myths in their heads. One of them is that asexual people can't get married. And even if they do, it will be an unsuccessful marriage. What makes people assume this?

There are many couples where the partners are not asexual, but still they don't have sex. Does that mean that there is no love in the relationship?

A romantic relationship between two non-asexual persons can start on a very sexual note. They might have sex all the time. However, with time they get used to each other and the frequency of sex reduces. Does that mean that there is no love?

If you ask a married couple that has been married for say 40 years, they might tell you that they have not had sex in years. This could be because of various reasons. There could be health reasons or age-related reasons or no reason at all. Yet, this couple could be inseparable. Both of them can't do a minute without each other, and sex has no role to play in this. It is possible to love and receive love without being sexually active.

You can't just rule out the possibility of love in a relationship that has no sex. Love is a very intimate feeling. Nobody can decide it for another person as to what should love mean to them.

Asexuality And Attraction

You might battle a thought in your head about how a person can be in love without any attraction whatsoever. How would he or she know whom to marry? If there is attraction, does that mean an asexual can marry anyone? Shouldn't some feeling be involved?

Yes, love has a lot to do with attraction. You get attracted to a person's beauty. You get attracted to the way they speak and carry themselves. You get attracted to their caring nature, thoughts, etc.

There are many kinds of attractions apart from sexual attraction. People only attempt to understand the latter, hence leading to all this confusion of sex and love.

While sexual attraction has a role to play in love, it is not the only thing required for love. An asexual person does not feel attraction at the sexual level, but he or she can get attracted to another person.

Romantic attraction plays its part when two people fall in love with each other. This is the kind attraction that keeps the two people in love and makes them feel that they want to be together.

Romantic attraction and sexual attraction are two separate things. If you are in a relationship with a person with whom you enjoy having sex and also wish to spend your life with them, then your romantic and sexual attraction are towards that person.

These two kinds of attractions can exist in absence of each other. A person can be sexually attracted to a person and yet not feel any romantic attraction. Such a person will only aim for a one-night stand or maybe a fling that involves sex.

In extramarital affairs where the man or woman is in love with his or her spouse, but still sleeps around with other men and women, this is a classic example of romantic attraction and sexual attraction being directed in different directions.

If you look around, you will find numerous examples of couples who fall into such kinds of arrangements. Some are only sexually attracted to each other, some are only romantically attracted to each other, some are both romantically and sexually attracted to each other.

An asexual person definitely falls in the category of people that can be romantically attracted to another person. There is no sexual attraction, but the romantic attraction is enough to initiate and sustain love.

Now, you would question as to whether an asexual person will fall in love with a man or a woman. There is no rule that all asexuals should get romantically attracted to members of the same sex or the opposite sex.

There are different types of sexual orientations. In the same way, there are different types of romantic orientations. The romantic orientation of a person will allow you to know whether he or she gets romantically attracted to a man or woman.

Romantic Orientations

By now you might have understood that there are many kinds of sexual orientation. Asexuality is also a kind of sexual orientation. Heterosexual, homosexual and bisexual are other kinds of sexual orientations.

The sexual orientation of a person tells you which gender the person feels sexually attracted to, if they feel any sexual attraction at all in their body.

Along similar lines, the romantic orientation of a person tells you which gender the person feels romantically attracted to, if at all.

Aromantic

Aromantic orientation is when a person does not get romantically attracted to anybody.

Heteroromantic

Heteroromantic orientation is when a person is romantically attracted to another person of the opposite gender.

Homoromantic

Homoromantic orientation is when a person is romantically attracted to another person of the same gender.

Biromantic

Biromantic orientation is when a person can be romantically attracted to a person of any of the two genders. Biromantic orientation is also referred to as panromantic orientation.

If you are an asexual man, you can be heteroromantic, homoromantic, biromantic or even aromantic. If you are an aromantic asexual, then you will neither experience sexual attraction nor romantic attraction.

There are some people who use shorthand names to refer to various orientations. For example, these people refer to heteroromantic asexual as a straight asexual.

Along similar lines, homoromantic asexual becomes either gay asexual or asexual lesbian. These terms are easier to write and pronounce, but many asexuals don't like using these shorthand terms.

It should be noted that you will not suddenly discover in which category of romantic orientation you fall. It might take a while for you to discover your romantic orientation. However, there is nothing to worry about because many people go through the same. They feel like they are somewhere in between two kinds of orientations. You can take your time.

For example, there are many asexuals who feel like they are somewhere in between an aromantic and a heteroromantic. It is not clear to them from their limited experiences as to where they fall.

These people might have been drawn towards members of the opposite sex but then it might not have felt right. This leads to confusion in the mind of the person.

You should not beat yourself up if you are also in a confused state. It is fine to be in this state. What is important is that you don't dismiss your feelings away.

If you are feeling something, then you are feeling it. It always pays to acknowledge your feelings. Acknowledge your feelings, even if you feel something else the very next moment. Just be true to yourself.

It is important to understand your experiences and find a common link between them to be able to discover where you actually belong.

Aesthetic Attraction

Along with sexual attraction and romantic attraction, a person can also feel aesthetic attraction. This kind of attraction also plays a part when a person is falling in love with another person.

When a person gets attracted by the looks of another person, it is termed as aesthetic attraction. The definition makes it sound as if aesthetic attraction and sexual attraction are the same, but this is not true. Aesthetic attraction is different to sexual attraction. They are very much different from each other.

A sexual attraction is accompanied by a thought to get sexual with the other person. When you are sexually attracted to another person, you wish to get physically intimate with a person.

When you find a person hot and sexy, it is more of a sexual attraction. On the other hand, when you find the other person beautiful and cute, there is aesthetic attraction.

An aesthetic attraction is more like describing the beauty of a landscape. The way you would choose to admire a beautiful landscape, the same way you see and describe the person to whom you are aesthetically attracted.

When you attempt to understand these two kinds of attractions, you will be able to figure out how an asexual can be attracted to the looks of another person, and yet not feel any sexual attraction.

As an asexual person, when you feel aesthetic attraction towards someone, it will not be accompanied by any sexual thoughts. You will not have this desire to get into bed with that person.

It is not necessary that aesthetic attraction leads to thoughts of love. Aesthetic attraction will only define your attraction towards the way the other person looks.

You might not even care to talk to the other person, and you will definitely not dream or wish to see the other person naked. That is sexual attraction. On the other hand, for a non-asexual person, his aesthetic attraction might be followed by a strong sexual desire.

Finding A Partner

The asexual person has no special way of finding a partner. They don't have a radar with which they send special signals. It is just like every other person finds a partner.

They meet people just like anyone else. If a person strikes a chord with them, they decide to meet them again. They might slowly fall in love with that person. That love might sustain or it might not. It is also important to note here that it is not necessary that an asexual person will only fall for another asexual person. Asexual people can fall in love and have successful relationships even with non-asexuals.

Asexual people can fall in love as normally as anyone else. There is no guarantee how long the relationship will last. This is also pretty much normal. A person falls in love, but how long the love remains is dependent on various other factors.

The asexual person can be in a fulfilling relationship. If it works well for both the partners, they can even go ahead and marry each other. This is the most normal thing for a couple that is in love.

Asexual people will do all the normal things that partners do. They have no special way of living or no code that needs to be cracked. They will also look for comfort and love in a relationship.

They will go out for dates and picnics; they will share their secrets and inhibitions; they will plan surprise birthdays for their partner; they might want to move in together; they might even want to get married and have babies together.

Would An Asexual Bcome Sexually Inclined After Falling In Love?

The disinterest of an asexual person in sex is not a temporary phase. It is not like it is a disease that will suddenly vanish after a certain something happens.

Irrespective of whether an asexual person is in love or not, they will not be sexually attracted to another person.

Even after living ten years with the same person, they will feel the same way. They will have no desire to be sexually intimate. They might have sex if that works for the couple, but the asexual is always better without it.

The couple might find of a way that suits them the best. They might decide not to have sex, or they might decide to have it sometimes. It is a personal call that the couple will have to take. However, love or marriage or divorce… nothing can really change a person's orientation. You might spend half of your life believing that you are of a certain orientation, but you might discover after years that you were always some other orientation.

Whether you discover your sexual and romantic orientation, or you ignore it, or you choose to believe that you are something else, you can't change your natural inclinations. It is not possible.

Relationships Between Two Asexual People

Most asexual people go through a phase of confusion and self-doubt. They will doubt their ability to function as a normal human being. If you are also battling through such a phase then you should know that this is very normal. There are many people out there who are going through such phases.

All you need is the right information so that you can access and analyze for yourself. Asexual people don't just get a sudden awakening that they are asexual; it is a realization that comes when you make an attempt to understand your sexual orientation in a better light. It is seen that asexual people doubt their ability to function as normal human beings.

There are people out there who would not believe that a relationship between two asexuals work. Wouldn't it be boring? Wouldn't it lack passion? How can such a relationship work?

Relationships between two asexual people can be great, in spite of what other people might think. Asexual people are not boring people by nature. They just don't sit and do nothing all day. They also have a life that they live in the most normal of ways. They will go out in the same manner as other people. They will wait for weekends like other people. They will do what everybody else does.

The definition of fun and excitement is different for such people, but they have their own ways to have fun. Asexual people could actually have more satisfactory relationships than the relationships of non-asexual people.

If you are an asexual person, then finding another asexual person could be your dream. You might think that such a person will get you and you will be more comfortable with them. You are right and also wrong if this is what you believe. Yes, an asexual person will get your views in sexuality because they would have similar views. They would also have faced many awkward situations in life owing to their asexuality. Similar thoughts and experiences will bring you closer and will help you to understand each other well. You will understand when your partner says that he or she doesn't want to have sex and only wishes to cuddle.

This will allow you to have a lot of freedom of thought and expression. You don't have to fake it now. Why should you fake to enjoy sex when you don't have to impress your partner? You are anyways in the same boat.

You will be able to spend your time on better things, things that you enjoy more. You will not have to waste time making the other person understand your take on sexuality. This can be very liberating for any person.

To be able to be free is the dream of every asexual. Asexual people are faced with so many assumptions and questions that they can get suffocated. They need people who would allow them to be what they wish to be.

Such a relationship can be very liberating. It will help you in your personal growth also. You don't have to spend your entire time and energy on explaining to people about your sexual orientation. There are other things to do as well.

When you are with a partner who gets you, you can focus on things that you enjoy and things that will help you to grow in your lives. You both can contribute to each other's personal growth.

On the other hand, their asexuality is not a guarantee that you guys will have the smoothest run. For a relationship to be successful, there are many factors that play a role. While you might get along on the asexuality factor, there are other factors also. A relationship needs emotional compatibility for it to work. They need to value each other for their struggles, victories and failures.

While your asexual partner will understand your struggle as an asexual, do you connect at a deeper level? Do you have other things that keep you connected except that fact that you both are asexual?

A thing that needs to be noted here is that just because two asexual people are in a relationship, that does not mean that there will be no challenges for them as a couple. Don't two bisexuals have challenges when they are in a relationship?

The two asexual people could have very different personalities. This will have an effect on the relationship. There is a chance that the two people can't get along on various other issues in their lives.

If you are asexual, then you know that your asexual partner will understand your sexual orientation. He or she will be able to understand your views towards sexual activities because he or she shares similar views.

But, these views could also vary a lot. No two asexual people will have the same mind. While one might abhor sex, the other might be okay with having it sometimes. While one might want to experiment with various sex positions, the other might never want to have it.

So, even if you are in a relationship with an asexual person, you will have to make sure that you are on the same page. Understand his or her thoughts and views and also share your views. This will help you to come to a common ground.

Chapter 9. The Ace Umbrella

Asexuality falls on a spectrum called as the ace spectrum. To understand asexuality, it is better to understand the other elements of this spectrum. It is also important to understand the distinctions between these elements.

This chapter will help you to understand the meaning and importance of the Ace Umbrella. This will aid your understanding of asexuality as an important part of the spectrum.

What Is The Ace Umbrella?

The Ace Umbrella is the gray area between sexuality and asexuality. If you dig deeper into the study of asexuality, you will understand that there are many people who are asexual by their sexual orientation, but still experience sexual attraction sometimes.

This is enough to confuse a person trying to understand their sexuality. How can an asexual person experience sexual attraction at times? Well, this section will help you understand such instances.

Asexuality is said to fall under an Ace Umbrella. The umbrella encompasses asexuality and various other orientations closely related to asexuality.

A person is said to be gray-asexual if he or she experiences sexual attraction sometimes. This might not be too frequent and not too strong a sensation.

The person will not have a very deep and uncontrollable desire. The sexual attraction will be so mild that it is confusing as to whether a person is feeling it or not.

There is a subtype of gray-asexual people known as demi-sexual. A demi-sexual will only experience sexual attraction when he or she is emotionally intimate and comfortable with the other person, which is characterized by a strong emotional bond with the person.

The reason to have these types in the Ace Umbrella is that these people are more similar to asexuals rather than non-asexuals. Such people will not be able to identify with the culture that homosexuals and heterosexuals belong to.

These people don't feel that strong sexual attraction most of the time like the non-asexuals. They are not driven and motivated by sex like the latter. This makes it obvious that they identify more with asexuals.

If you ask about the sexual experiences of gray-asexuals and demisexuals, you will see that they have experiences similar to asexuals. They feel as alienated as asexual people when the non-sexual ones boast about their sexual endeavors.

They are also called as asexuals with exceptions because of the fact that they can feel sexual attraction sometimes. They have a few exceptions, but otherwise are quite asexual in their orientation. You might also be interested in knowing the time period for which the gray-asexuals and demisexuals can go without sex or even sexual attraction. They can actually go without either for years. It is really difficult to separate them from asexual people.

Gray-asexuality

Gray-asexuality is basically for all those people who are confused between being an asexual and a non-asexual. People who feel that they are somewhere in the middle, but more towards asexuals are actually gray-asexuals.

There are no strict rules that you need to abide by. Gray-asexuality is a way to define the gray area that lies between asexuality and non-asexuality. It is like that area where two colors get mixed.

When you mix the two colors, there are some areas that show more prominence of one color, and there are some areas that show prominence of the other one. Gray-asexuality is also like that. It is more about the area where asexuality and non-asexuality get mixed. It is not a separating line, but a gray-area.

If you have felt sexual attraction even once in your life, you can't be an asexual. An asexual will not feel any sexual attraction whatsoever. Gray-asexuality is an attempt to define the confusion that resides between the zone of asexuality and non-asexuality.

There are many gray-asexuals that have experienced sexual attraction only once or twice in their entire life. There are many gray-asexuals who experience a feeling that they think is sexual attraction, but they themselves are not very sure.

For most gray-asexuals, the sexual feelings are so bleak that sometimes they question themselves whether it actually happened or not. For some, the feelings are controllable and any distraction can stop them.

Most gray-asexuals enjoy sex, but they don't crave it very badly. They can happily live without it.

As mentioned earlier, gray-asexuality has been included in the Ace Umbrella to take care of all the ambiguities and confusions, but one thing is for sure that gray-asexuals are more asexuals than non-asexuals.

Difference between gray-asexuals, demisexuals and non-asexuals

You might also argue that even non-asexuals don't feel sexual attraction every minute of the day. Their area of focus could be sex, but they will also only get attracted to a few people, depending on their orientation.

Sexual attraction will always vary from person to person. You might feel sexually attracted to one person and I might feel it for someone else. In terms of frequency, you might be more active than me.

Non-asexuals are not sexually attracted to other people all the time, but they are attracted many a times. This sexual attraction could be a constant feeling towards a romantic interest. It could also be towards someone the person likes in the office or college. It might be devoid of any romantic inclination whatsoever. It could also be that weird feeling when you look at a poster of your favorite celebrity.

It is not necessary to act on the sexual attraction. It will not increase or decrease your sexual orientation. The presence of sexual attraction is enough to define your sexual orientation. This is where the non-asexuals differentiate from gray-asexuals and demisexuals. The latter don't function this way. They are not harbored by a constant sexual attraction towards anybody. For gray-asexuals and demisexuals, they might have experienced this feeling of sexual attraction only to a single person in all their life. It is also possible that they haven't felt so in years.

Does Demisexuality Mean That The Person Is Very Choosy About Their Partners?

When we say that demisexuals can feel sexually attracted only towards someone they share a very intimate bond with, it can raise a question in the minds of many people. People might believe that demisexuals are those choosy and picky people that believe in only one partner. They believe in only having sexual interactions with the one they truly love.

Demisexuality should not be confused with the morality of a person. What a person feels about sex and love on a moral ground is a very different topic. If a person is demisexual, it does not imply that he or she is waiting for the right person to have sex with. It also does not mean that her or she is trying to act superior to those who have sexual interactions with random people.

The person is not trying to portray a picture of a saint or even trying to suppress inner feelings about sex – they just work that way.

As explained in a previous chapter, what a person chooses to do is their plan of action and behavior. If he or she has an urge to do something, it is their choice to act on that urge or not.

What demisexuals choose to do is not the topic of study here. We are trying to define their sexual attraction. They are sexually attracted to only those with whom they are emotionally bonded.

It is also not necessary that they are sexually attracted to everyone they are emotionally close to. If at all they experience sexual attraction, it will be to someone who is emotionally close to them. This is the simplest way to define demisexuality.

Again, a demisexual could be a virgin. The demisexual could have had sex a few times. It is also possible that the demisexual has had sex several times with different partners.

What the demisexual does is a personal choice. You can have sex even without feeling sexual attraction. Demisexuality as a sexual orientation only defines how a person with this sexual orientation will feel sexually stimulated and attracted. Their morality and actual sexual activity are totally different topics.

It should also be noted that the emotional intimacy that is being discussed here is not necessarily a love bond. It is important not to confuse emotional intimacy with love. Love will have emotional intimacy, but emotional intimacy is not necessarily love.

Romantic orientations of demisexual and gray-asexual

Asexuals can have different types of romantic orientations. In the same way, the demisexuals and gray-asexuals can also have different kinds of romantic orientations. It is even possible for demisexuals and gray-asexuals to be aromantic. An aromantic person will not be romantically oriented towards any other person.

A person can be demiromantic or gray-romantic. A person is said to be gray-romantic if he or she experiences romantic attraction sometimes. This might not be too frequent and not too strong a feeling. A demiromantic will only experience romantic attraction when he or she is emotionally intimate and comfortable with the other person, which is characterized by a strong emotional bond with the person.

There are various kinds of orientations possible. For example, a person can also be panromantic gray-asexual or a hetroromantic demisexual.

Differentiating asexual from demisexual and gray-asexual

It can be a bit challenging to understand how you can distinguish between a demisexual, gray-asexual and an asexual. What is the exact formula? The truth is that there is no formula for this.

Most asexuals will have this doubt that what if they believe that are asexual, then someday they realize that they were demi or gray. The possibility of this happening can't be ruled out.

If you have not faced sexual attraction up to an age, there is no formula that can prove that you will never face it. You can face it tomorrow. This is why the Ace Umbrella is defined. It helps to group the experiences of people who are definitely not non-asexuals.

The best way to deal with this complication is to take things as they come your way. Don't force yourself into anything. Don't force yourself to feel sexual attraction, because this can never happen with force.

In the same way, don't force yourself to not feel sexual attraction. If after years of believing that you are an asexual, you feel sexual attraction, accept it. Don't rule this out. Accept that maybe you were always a demisexual. Every demisexual or gray-asexual will feel sexual attraction towards another person for the very first time. It will be confusing for them, but the best way to deal with it is to accept it.

Don't put yourself in a bracket. Be open and understand your experiences in a better way. Nothing that you are feeling is wrong. You just need to understand what you are feeling and what that implies in your life.

Chapter 10.   Symbols That Represent Asexuality

There are a few symbols that have been adopted over the years to represent asexuals. The aim of these symbols is to show solidarity and respect for each other. Asexuals are also sexual minorities and it is important to raise a voice for their rights. It is important to understand that they are as normal as any other person walking on the street.

These symbols go a long way in uniting sexual minorities across the world. People make use of these symbols to show their support in various marches and even in their everyday lives. This chapter will help you to understand the various symbols that are used all across the world to represent asexuality. People are slowly becoming conscious of all the ignored minorities in the world.

Asexuality Flag

There is an asexuality flag that stands for all the asexuals of the world. This flag is also called as the ace flag. The ace flag is one of the most popular symbols of asexuality.

The flag was designed in a way to keep it as simple as possible and was adopted with open hearts by all the asexuals of the world after it was unveiled.

Before the flag was decided as the symbol of asexuality, asexuals around the world used other symbols to extend support to each other and to feel united. The symbols used were a heart that is half filled and an AVEN triangle.

The AVEN (Asexuality Visibility and Education Network) triangle was used because it was the symbol of a popular website that many asexuals affiliated themselves too. But, not all asexuals were subscribed to it, so a symbol that was more universal was required.

The problem with the heart was that many asexuals believed that the heart was used as a symbol of love and romance. Many aromantic asexuals did not feel a part of a group like this, so again there was a need for something better.

It was decided to design and adopt a flag that stood for all asexuals around the world and also for all kinds of asexuals. In 2010, the users of the AVEN website led a mission to come up with a more unifying symbol of asexuality.

Many websites dedicated to asexuality took part in this mission all over the world. There were many suggestions for the design of the flag and a voting system was set up to determine the ultimate winner.

The majority of people chose the current design as their choice. Finally, the flag from the proposed design was created by AVEN and the asexuality flag was posted on the Internet on 30th June, 2010.

The current flag for asexuality does not have a symbol. It was consciously avoided because different symbols can mean different things to various people. It was a conscious effort to keep the design simple, as a simple design makes it easier to be recognized and adopted. It was also important that the flag does not show affiliation to any religion or country. The current flag is simple, yet meaningful for all asexuals.

Each of the four colors of the flag stands for something. The top black stripe in the flag stands for asexuality. The second stripe that is painted in gray stands for gray-asexuality and demisexuality. The third stripe that is painted in white stands for non-asexual partners and also allies. The fourth stripe that is painted in purple stands for community.

The use of the ace flag as the symbol of asexuality is very popular and there are clothes, stickers and buttons that carry the flag of asexuality. Many asexual bloggers use the design of the flag in their website design. People use the four colors in various forms to show their asexuality and the flag is used in various parades that stand for sexual minorities. The flag design is used by asexuals in various forms, such as book covers, hoardings headbands and bracelets.

Black Rings

Another symbol that asexuals around the world have taken over is the black ring. If a person is wearing a black ring on the right hand, it is to signify that he or she is an asexual. The ring is worn on the middle finger.

Contrary to what people might believe, the middle finger has no relevance in the choice of finger for asexuals. Even the color black has no real meaning in this regard, it just happens that the middle finger and the black color are chosen.

The color of the ring should be something that people don't find too loud. The color black is one of the most neutral colours and it can be worn with anything and everything. So, it was decided as the color of the ring.

One of the main reasons to choose the right hand and the middle finger was that if the ring was worn on the left finger, it could signify an engagement or marriage ring in many cultures. So, to keep the confusion at bay, the right hand was chosen.

The material of the ring can be a personal choice. There is no regulation on that. The ring can be as simple as possible. It can be made of stainless steel, plastic or any other material of choice.

Most asexuals around the world choose a simple band of black as the ring. There are some asexuals who also go for the symbol of ace on the black ring. Some also choose fancier rigs with gray and purple highlights on the black.

The black ring was chosen in June 2005 as one of the official symbols of asexuality.

Cake

Another symbol of asexuality that has been adopted all over the world is the cake. This might come as a surprise to many people, but there is actually a significance attached to the adoption of this symbol.

Asexuals are not secret bakers. They are not trying to promote the cakes of their bakery or some other bakery. Asexuals believe and take pride in the fact that cake is better than sex. Though this is a symbol of asexuality, many non-asexuals will also agree on this statement. Some asexuals also believe that pie is clearly better than cake. They consider pie as the perfect symbol of asexuality.

Chapter 11. Celibacy And Abstinence

There is a lot of confusion that surrounds celibacy, abstinence and asexuality, and people like to believe that all these terms are interchangeable.

If you have always enjoyed sex, but for some reason or another you haven't had sex in the past few weeks or months or even years, then do you suddenly change into an asexual person?

No, you have probably become celibate because it is not possible to turn into an asexual. It is importance to understand what celibacy and abstinence are. How are they similar or different to asexuality?

There are many people that believe that there is a group of people who don't want to have sex. They hate sex for some reason. But, they want to fit in and appear cool, so they have coined the word asexuality.

These people definitely don't have any idea of what celibacy and abstinence are. They just like to believe that celibacy and abstinence are all fancy terms that essentially mean 'say no to sex'.

This chapter will help you to understand celibacy and abstinence so that you can understand asexuality in better light. The next time someone tries to argue with you that all three are the same, you would know that it is the ignorance of the person that is speaking.

Celibacy And Asexuality

It is important to understand celibacy and how it is different to asexuality. Celibacy defines the behavior of a person in regards to sexual activities. On the other hand, asexuality is the sexual orientation of the person.

A person who is celibate will not be having sex because of a specific reason. It can't be assumed that an asexual person is not having sex. An asexual person will not have the sexual attraction towards anybody, but the person could still be having sex. Who are we to stop them? Nobody will question them or decide that he or she should not be in the community anymore.

There are many people who believe that celibacy and asexuality are similar concepts. They stand for not having sex. The only difference is that the former defines not having sex voluntarily and the latter defines not having sex involuntarily.

These people believe that the celibate decides not to have sex, while the poor asexual just can't have sex. This is not true at all. Celibacy is the behavior of not having sex. It is also important to understand here that it is not necessary that celibacy is always a choice. It may or may not be a choice of the person. We can't assume anything on this part.

If a person is in jail, he or she can't have sex because the circumstances don't allow them. If given a chance, the person would definitely have sex. This means that the person is not having sex due to circumstances and not choice.

If a person lives in New York and their partner stays in Bombay, they are forced to not have sex because of the distance. The day they'll get a chance, they will have sex. If a person is not well and has not had sex in months, this makes them celibate. Yet, it should be noted that here again it is not the choice of the person. The day they feel better, they will start to want sex again.

You should also understand how far asexuality and celibacy can be related. It is important to understand that an asexual person can be celibate, but there is the probability that he or she is not. The asexual person will not have any sexual attraction towards anybody. In spite of that, if he or she has sex, then they re not a celibate. On the other hand, if he or he does not have sex, he or she is an asexual and a celibate.

Abstinence

As explained in the previous section, celibacy may or may not be a choice of the person. Abstinence is defined as the behavior of not having sex as a choice.

In the case of abstinence, we know that it is the choice of the person to not have sex. There are no environmental or social reasons that are behind this decision of not having sex.

The person could have had sex several times in the past, but if he or she gives it up by choice, he or she is an abstinent. There could be religious, social or personal reasons behind this decision that the person has taken.

Asexuality is not taken up because of any religious, social or personal reason. A person can't take up asexuality like one can take up abstinence. A person is asexual or not.

Celibacy means not having sex, with or without choice, and abstinence is not having sex with choice. So, a person who is abstinent is also celibate. On the other hand, a person who is celibate may or may not be abstinent.

An asexual person can be abstinent. The asexual person will not have any sexual attraction towards anybody. In spite of that, if they have sex, they are not abstinent. On the other hand, if he or she chooses not have sex because of a social, personal or religious reason, they are asexual and abstinent.

Chapter 12. Some Useful Tips For Asexuals

While you are trying to understand asexuality, it is important that you learn how an asexual person's brain works. Again, each person is different. They will act and behave more so because of their experiences and knowledge, and less so because of their sexuality.

However, understanding one's sexuality also has an effect on a person. This understanding also helps to develop certain personality traits. This chapter has been designed based on how different asexual people have felt or experienced.

It will give you a glimpse into the mind of an asexual person. When an asexual person is dealing with the identity crisis of understanding why he or she is so different from others, he or she will have various thoughts.

All those people who are trying to understand their sexuality should understand various topics related to asexuality with precision. This will help them to feel more confident and better about themselves.

Imagine that you find traits of asexuality in you and also enjoy masturbation. This scenario can confuse even an asexual person. He or she will feel like they has an identity crisis and does not fit in anywhere.

Based on how an asexual person feels and functions, various tips and tricks have been discussed. These tips help you lead a better life and also have better and meaningful relationships.

Accepting Your Asexuality Will Help To Know What You Really Want

Another very interesting aspect of asexuality is that it will help you to really know what you want out of a relationship. You will be a better judge of your wants and needs when you get into a relationship with someone.

Many a times, people are so blinded by sex that there is nothing else they look for in a relationship. They will chase sex and everything that they do will revolve around it.

Haven't you heard stories of people cheating and dumping each other because of sex? People disappoint their partners and cheat on them only to get some sex out of the relationship. Their lives revolve around this one thing.

You don't want sex. Doesn't that make your life simpler? You don't have to cheat on anyone just to get some satisfaction in bed. If you think, you actually have a better chance of forming more meaningful relationships.

Now when sex is already out of the picture, you will have to look at other things that will help you form a meaningful relationship. You should utilize this opportunity and understand what it is that you really want.

You don't have to fight sexual urges like most other people. Shouldn't you be using this fact of your advantage? Doesn't this give you extra time to look into yourself and analyze your needs as an individual?

Are you looking for a deeper connection? Do you just want somebody to talk to? Do you feel the need to share a life with somebody? Are you only looking for a good friend?

You can only offer something in a relationship when you know what you want out of it. Be clear what you are looking for. Enjoy your asexuality and understand yourself in a better light.

Don't compromise on your asexuality

You should always remember that there is no need to compromise your asexuality for anybody. The person who doesn't accept you the way you are is not worth having.

While compromises are a part of relationships, but a compromise on your asexuality should be the last thing on your mind. This is not something that can be given up or cured. You will lose if you fight such a battle.

If you accept your partner for his or her sexual orientation, shouldn't he or she do the same? Yes, it is important to find a common ground and come to a solution that works well for both of you, but if your partner wants you to be more sexually active and behave like you are a non-asexual, then this is a big problem. You can't expect your partner to behave like an asexual person, so how can your partner expect such things from you?

It is important that you know where you should draw the line. Make an attempt to understand how your partner understands things, but also make an attempt to make him or her see the way you see things.

You can form meaningful relationships when you are accepted and valued for what you add to the relationship. Having unreal expectations or trying to fulfill unreal expectations will not take the bond anywhere.

Educate yourself

It is not an easy world for asexual people. Firstly, the social setup makes it very difficult for the asexual to know of their asexuality. If people of the world were more comfortable with asexuality, wouldn't it be easier for people to learn about their sexual orientation?

If people spoke about asexuality as much as they speak about sex, wouldn't it be easier for people to understand asexuality? Shouldn't a young adult know about asexuality? Why is his or her mind fed only with sex?

Sex is everywhere. You can find it on television, movies, books, magazines and day-to-day conversations. Where is asexuality? Nobody talks about it.

This setup makes it very difficult for a person who doesn't feel like homosexuals or heterosexuals. If you are one of those people who are trying to figure out why you feel different, then you need to educate yourself as much as possible.

Read about asexuality and apply it to all the experiences that you have had. You will feel better and more confident when you realize that you have been normal all along. The battle does not end once you discover that you are an asexual. You would come to a point where you would have to come out and let people know of your asexuality. This could be a real task for anyone.

You should come out as and when and if you think it to be right. You should understand that this is an important part and you should not do it in a jiffy.

Education is the greatest tool to deal with any adversity. If you educate yourself, you will go a long way in helping yourself gain back all the confidence that you might have lost.

Read as much as you can about your sexuality. In addition, take out time to read about the sexuality of your partner. Make an attempt to understand how your partner understands things. Compare it with your understanding.

If you have friends that are asexual, you should take the time to connect with them. Talk about your thoughts and joke about things. You will love it when you are in the company of people who think and function like you.

Connect with other asexual people online. Look for any groups that you can join. This will help you to know that you are not alone. You will understand that it is as normal to be asexual as anything else.

When you listen to the experiences of other people, you will be able to analyze your own experiences. You will understand what all other asexual people are going through.

There are many blogs on the Internet that are maintained by asexual people. They share their experiences and thoughts on these blogs. Read such blogs and also share your own experiences.

Tips to have better relationships

Human beings dwell on human relationships. What is the purpose of a life if there are no meaningful relationships in it? We all want to healthy and fulfilling relations.

If you have discovered that you are an asexual person, then you will come to a stage where you will worry about the romantic relationships that you can have. You will have many doubts and questions.

As an asexual person, can you never get close and intimate with anyone? Can you never reach a point where you are comfortable and still yourself in a relationship? Will you always have to fake your way through a relationship?

These doubts are legitimate, and you will have to address them sooner or later. If you are not asexual but are in a relationship with an asexual person, even then you will have to understand asexuality and its effects on relationships.

Any kind of sexuality will have an effect on the relationship that you are having. Asexuality is no different. It will have its effect on your understanding of things, which will further affect your relationships.

It should be noted that it might have an effect on all your relationships, but the affect is more prominent and severe in cases of romantic relationships.

The sexuality of both the partners will have an affect on each other. A relationship is not just built on the foundation of sexual interactions. If you can work on other things, such as love and trust, you can go a long way in ensuring that you have fulfilling relationships.

Asexuality does not make you a lesser person

All the attention and hype that comes with sex has made us believe that it is the must have attribute in everyone's life. Sex and sex talks are everywhere. Too much importance is given to it.

Nobody ever taught us when we grew up that it is okay not to be too excited about sex and everything that relates to it. This is the biggest problem, and we need to work our way out of this.

You have to know that sex does not add or take away from the person that you are. Your personality and identity is not dependent on your sexual activities that you indulge in or don't indulge in.

Help yourself to come out of this rut. You are as good as anybody else. You are as capable of having meaningful relationships as anybody else. If you don't believe in yourself, then no one else will.

Be open and honest

An asexual person can get very conscious of the way he or she looks at sexual activities. If you don't deal with your insecurities, they will get the better of you even before you realize it. You will start avoiding confrontations and loathing other people.

Irrespective of your sexual orientation, it is your responsibility to be honest to yourself. You have to accept the facts for what they are. There is no use faking things because that will not get you anywhere.

If you fake being a person with a different sexuality, how will that benefit you? You will only turn into something that you are not. You might fake to make your partner believe that you enjoy sex. But, wouldn't your partner finally know that you are not enjoying sex? Doesn't your partner deserve to know the real you? Wouldn't you just get tired of not being you?

The question really is how long can you fake to be somebody else? Wouldn't you be finally caught? If you don't enjoy a certain sandwich, why should you pretend to enjoy it? It is not your problem that other people enjoy it.

It is critical that you are open and honest in your dealings with others. Tell your partner with utmost honesty how you feel. He or she has the right to know the real you. Would you like if your partner hid a significant truth about themself from you?

Everybody appreciates honesty in any relationship. The other person might take some time to understand your thought cycle, but that is okay. You can give them that time.

There should be no shame in being oneself. You are what you are. Accept yourself. This is the only way that others will accept you. Nobody can understand a person who refuses to understand themself.

Relationship with your family

It is also important to have a good relationship with your family. If you have someone in your family who understands you and whom you can trust, things will always get easier for you.

Everybody has a different family setup. You know your family the best. Some families are not open to discussions about sexuality. On the other hand, there are many others who are completely okay with it.

You should do what feels right for you. If you have a support system in the family then you will find it easier to deal with the world.

Try to initiate some open discussions with your family. Talk to them about your thoughts when you find the right opportunity. Tell them about things that they don't understand. This will make your life better.

Don't waste your time being insecure about your asexuality. This is nothing but a waste of time. We should be ashamed of ourselves when we do something wrong. Asexuality has no right or wrong, so why this shame?

Form good bonds with friends

You might be surprised to know that as an asexual person, you actually have a better chance of forming more meaningful friendships. This does not mean that other people can't have meaningful relationships, but you will have your advantages. Members of the opposite sex will feel more comfortable with you. They will be able to share things with you without any inhibitions.

For example, if you are an asexual man, then women will feel comfortable and free in your presence because they know that you are not fantasizing about them in your head.

They will know that you don't objectify them and you don't want to end up in bed with them after all your friendly gestures. This is a great opportunity to form meaningful bonds with other people.

You can focus on knowing the other person well. Sex will not be a roadblock because that is not even there in your mind. Things would be simpler and less complicated. Isn't this the ideal scenario for a great friendship?

Having a good set of friends will also help you to accept yourself in a better way. They will encourage you and love you for what you are. Share your thoughts with them and feel free with them. Friends can add great value to your life.

You should always try to form such good bonds where you have the freedom to be yourself. Understand what people have to say, and also feel free to share how you see the world. Your friends will only appreciate you.

Another interesting thing that you might notice is that the more open you are about your asexuality, the better things get for you. You no longer have to hang out with people who don't understand you.

You will start attracting like-minded people who could be of a different sexual orientation, but they will have an open heart and mind to accept different kinds of people.

You will also notice that you attract a lot of intelligent and sensitive people who want to understand more about asexuality. They will encourage you to open up because it will help them to learn more.

Dating

Many asexual people have admitted that casual dating is tough for them. In today's world, when we talk about dating, we essentially talk about sex. There are few people who are okay with a simple lunch and dinner date not ending in sex.

Even if a date does not end in sex, at least one of the main motives of going on a date is to have sex. As you grow older, it only gets more complex. As a teen you would view dating differently, but as an adult, it would definitely be different.

Dating is complex for almost everybody. It is fun for most, but there are some conflicts of interests and some complications. It becomes all the more complex for asexuals.

You might find it hard to date. Your date might not hold the same idea of a date as yours. Many asexual persons have also admitted that when they are younger and sex is not the only reason to out with people, it is a little simpler.

If you are out of college and not that young, then you need to accept it the way it is. Invest your time in stronger friendships and relationships rather than disappointing dates. You have nothing to lose in this case.

If you are young and still in college, then everybody around you would still be figuring out the dating concept. They might be of a different sexual orientation than you, but even they would be part excited and part confused.

You could enjoy the phase if you wish to. Go out with people, hang out with them and get to know them better.

Learning to assess situations

It is important that you learn to analyze and understand various situations for what they are. This will be difficult in the beginning, and will only come with time, but once you know that you are asexual, be a little more prepared.

If you look back, you will remember many situations where someone was making a sexual advance on you, and you acted really dumb. You would understand when you were prey to stupid sexual comments.

When you educate yourself about asexuality, you will also understand your reactions in various situations. You will also be able to understand the situations from the point of view of other people.

This will help you to avoid such situations in the past. It will help you to be more aware of your surroundings. When you are confident of who you are and what you are, people will slowly learn to respect you.

Enjoy the freedom

There is no need to be scared once you have discovered that you are an asexual person. In fact, you should look at the positives.

There is a certain sense of freedom that will follow when you discover the answer to all your questions. All this while, you might be pretending to be bisexual, when you know that are an asexual and there so many like you; isn't that freedom?

You can choose to enjoy this freedom. Stop pretending to be someone else. Don't make attractions, even if you have done so in the past. Imagine how fun this can be. You no longer have to force yourself to hook up with people just to prove that you are normal. You are an asexual, and that is a different kind of normal.

While your friends are chasing others for sex, you can sit at home and enjoy yourself. You can go out for movies and dinners and come back to home to sleep. Isn't it a relief to get rid of all the drama that people do to get sex? Enjoy it.

Dealing with people's ignorance

There would be many people who would think that you are just trying to be different. This could come from even some of your closest people. You need to be prepared for blows like this.

People still don't understand what asexuality is. They will think it is some agenda that you are trying to bring up to gain attention. You should definitely try to educate such people and tell them what asexuality is about.

But, when you see people being closed to you and the idea of asexuality, then you should just give up. Leave such people in their ignorant worlds. You need to move on. People will surprise you with their ignorance all the time. Some asexual people have shared in their talks and blogs that their closest friends thought that in LGBTQIA, the A is for allies and not asexual.

According to such people, there is nothing known as asexual rights, and even if there are such rights, they are not important. These people don't understand how asexual people fall into sexual minorities.

You need to make a way to avoid such hurtful comments. People need to be more educated and informed. But, again that is not your problem. The best you can do is just work on yourself and get more informed.

Learn to deal with the loneliness

There might come a time when you will realize that you are not the priority of people. Your friends could be running after their crushes and love interests and others might be enjoying their random sexual encounters.

You might find that there are not many people who would want to hang out your way. It is not a good feeling to realize that you are not the priority of anyone, but you have to learn to deal with this.

Once you have discovered your asexuality, you should make an effort to understand what comes along with it. It is not necessary that you feel this way. You could have a great circle of friends.

But, there is a chance and it is better to be prepared about it. Your friends will eventually get married and will have their own families. Things will change drastically then because you might still be struggling with your sexuality issues.

You should develop some hobbies that you can do all alone, such as reading. Spend your time learning new things. This will give you more confidence.

You should also not give up. You should not give up the pursuit to look for people like you. You are not the only asexual person in the world. There are many more who are in the same boat as yours. Not all people function the same way. You might find someone who gels well with your personality, irrespective of his or her sexuality. You should keep looking. You never know who you can find.

Chapter 13. Glossary

This glossary will help you define and understand the terms that are commonly used in context with asexuality. It will help you when you need a quick reference for the various commonly used terms.

Abstinence: Abstinence is defined as the act of giving up sexual acts. This is a choice that a person makes owing to various personal reasons.

Ace: Ace is a colloquial abbreviation that is used for the term asexual. Gay is a colloquial abbreviation that is used to denote homosexual people. Similarly, the word straight is used for people that are heterosexual.

Ace spectrum: Demisexual, asexual and gray-asexual can be grouped together and can be referred to as the ace spectrum.

Aesthetic attraction: There are many kinds of attractions. An attraction can be sexual or asexual. An aesthetic attraction is defined as the attraction that one feels in a non-sexual and non-romantic way. When you feel attracted by someone in a non-romantic way, it is termed as aesthetic attraction.

Affectional orientation: It is the same as romantic orientation. The affectional orientation of a person is defined by describing which gender or genders he or she gets romantically inclined or attracted towards.

Anti-sexual: Anti-sexual and asexual are not the same thing, though some people might confuse them to be. Anti-sexual is hatred towards sexual activities. People who are anti-sexual dislike anything sexual and believe that sex is a bad thing.

A-romantic: The word a-romantic is used to denote people who do not feel a romantic inclination towards any of the genders.

Arousal: The word arousal in the sexual context is often referred to as the act of getting sexually turned on. This turning on signifies sexual attraction. It is categorized by a physical reaction by the genitals, such as lubrication and erection.

Asexuality: Asexuality is a type of sexual orientation. It defines the natural tendency of a person in terms of his or her sexuality. Asexual people are sexually not attracted to any gender. Being asexual is not a choice. You can't decide whether you wish to be asexual or not. You are either asexual or you are not.

Bi-romantic: Bi-romantic is a term that helps to establish the romantic inclination and orientation of a person who is romantically attracted to both the genders. Such a person will feel romantic feelings for both men and women.

Bisexual: Bisexual is a term that helps to establish the sexual orientation of a person who is sexually attracted to both the genders. Such a person will feel sexually attracted to both men and women.

Black ring: The black ring has become popular to signify the asexuality of a person. If you wear a black colored ring on your middle finger of right hand, you wish to state to the world that you are an asexual person with no interest in sexual activities whatsoever.

Celibacy: Celibacy is defined as the act of giving up sexual acts. There could be many reasons that could have made the person do so. This could be a personal choice, or there could be other reasons behind this.

Coming out: This particular phrase is used when a person decides to reveal something that he or she has been hiding. It is used when a person, irrespective of their sexual orientation, decided to reveal it to his or her family and friends. For example, you could come out and tell the world that you are an asexual.

Demi: Demi is widely used as an abbreviation for the term demisexual (see below).

Demiromantic: A person is said to be demiromantic if that person can only be romantically attracted to another person after they have already formed a strong and comfortable emotional bond. Emotional intimacy is the prerequisite for such people to feel love.

Demisexual: A demi-sexual will only experience sexual attraction when he or she is emotionally intimate and comfortable with the other person, which is characterized by a strong emotional bond with the person. Demisexuality has nothing to do with the morality of the person. Just because a person wants to have sex only after marriage does not mean he or she is demisexual. There is a subtype of gray-asexual people known as demi-sexual. The reason to have these types in the ace umbrella is that these people are more related to the asexuals rather than the non-asexuals.

Grace: Grace is widely used as an abbreviation for the term Gray-Asexual.

Gray-A: Gray-A is widely used as an abbreviation for the term Gray-Asexual.

Gray-Asexual: The word gray stands for the gray area that is between asexuality and non-asexuality. A person is said to be gray-asexual if he or she experiences sexual attraction sometimes. This might not be too frequent and not too strong a sensation. The person will not have a very deep and uncontrollable desire. The sexual attraction will be so mild that he or she would be confused whether they actually had it or not. These people don't feel that strong sexual attraction like non-asexuals. They are not driven and motivated by sex like the latter. This makes it obvious that they identify more with the asexuals.

Heteroromantic: Heteroromantic is a kind of romantic orientation that is characterized by a romantic inclination or attraction towards members of the opposite gender.

Heterosexual: Heterosexual is a kind of sexual orientation that is characterized by a sexual inclination or attraction towards members of the opposite gender.

Homoromantic: Homoromantic is a kind of romantic orientation that is characterized by a romantic inclination or attraction towards members of the same gender.

Homosexual: Homosexual is a kind of sexual orientation that is characterized by a sexual inclination or attraction towards members of the same gender.

Libido: Libido is also called the sex drive of a person. Libido causes a person to be sexually aroused. A high sex drive or libido in a person means that the person has a high desire and urge to indulge in a sexual activity.

Lithoromantic: A person is said to be Lithoromantic if he or she is capable of feeling romantic attraction, but has no desire to get any romance in reciprocation.

Panromantic: Panromantic is a kind of romantic orientation that is characterized by a romantic inclination or attraction towards members of any gender.

Pansexual: Pansexual is a kind of sexual orientation that is characterized by a sexual inclination or attraction towards members of any gender.

Romantic attraction: Romantic attraction is defined when a person desires to get intimate with a person on a romantic level.

Romantic orientation: Romantic orientation is defined by describing which gender or genders one gets romantically inclined or attracted towards.

Sexual attraction: Sexual attraction is defined when a person desires to get intimate with a person on a sexual level. In simpler words, a person wishes to have a sexual encounter with the person he or she is sexually attracted to.

Sexual orientation: Sexual orientation of a person is defined by describing which gender or genders he or she gets sexually inclined or attracted towards.

Conclusion

Thank you again for purchasing this book!

I hope this book was able to help you in understanding asexuality in a better light. There is a lot of confusion in the minds of people relating to how an asexual person leads his or her life. People find it difficult to accept that a person feels the way an asexual person does.

There are so many such questions that an asexual person is hounded with. It is important that all these questions are addressed, so that all the confusion can be removed. It is important for an asexual person to get comfortable with his or her sexual orientation. At the same time, it is also important for other people around them to understand things in a better perspective.

Asexuality is the absence of sexual attraction towards any of the genders in a person. Though the definition of asexuality is simple and straightforward, it might not be enough for a person who is trying to understand their sexuality. Each asexual person will differ from another asexual person, and this makes it all the more difficult. If you are trying to figure out whether you are asexual or not, it can be a real challenge. You will have to understand the idea of asexuality in depth to know whether you are asexual or not.

We are always told that sex is an important part of a relationship. This conditioning makes it very difficult for us to accept that things can be different. There is no denying this fact. Any kind of sexuality will have an effect on the relationship that you are having. You should know that asexuality is no different. It will have its effect on your understanding of things, which will further affect your relationships, but these effects need to be understood in a better way so that you are prepared for them. You should know what lies ahead of you on this road.

If you are confused about your sexuality, you definitely need to dig deep and understand things. This will help you to broaden your horizon and give you the confidence that you might have lost while you were trying to figure why you aren't like everybody else. Even if you are not asexual, you need to know about asexuality. You could have a friend or relative who could be battling with the various myths and confusions of asexuality. Your understanding of asexuality will help you to help them in their journey.

This book is meant to help you deal with everything that is related to asexuality. After reading this book, you will definitely realize that being asexual is not a defect or a disease. You don't need any treatment or cure. You just need to educate yourself and get comfortable with your sexuality. This book should have helped you to understand how an asexual person feels and how they have to deal with all the pressures of society. This will help you to realize that you are not alone and will also help you to prepare yourself for the road ahead. Various frequently asked questions have been answered and various myths have been debunked.

This book can be a life changer for you in many ways. Understanding your sexual orientation and getting comfortable is a huge step in changing your life for the better. The book is designed in a way that you can understand what goes on in the mind of an asexual person. This will help you to analyze your own thoughts and put them in perspective. The book will help you to keep away all the clouds of doubt that might be hanging around you.

Thank you and good luck!

References

Websites were all live at the time of going to press. This could change – and of course, is out of our control.

https://en.wikipedia.org

http://wiki.asexuality.org

http://www.whatisasexuality.com

http://time.com

http://www.wikihow.com

http://everydayfeminism.com

http://www.stop-homophobia.com

http://www.cosmopolitan.com

http://young.scot

https://www.psychologytoday.com

http://www.bbc.com/news

https://www.7cups.com

http://www.asexuality.org

http://www.telegraph.co.uk

https://www.youtube.com

http://www.refinery29.com

https://en.wiktionary.org

https://www.reddit.com

http://www.asexualityarchive.com

https://www.theguardian.com

https://www.stuff.co.nz

www.bbc.co.uk

http://nymag.com

https://rowman.com

http://www.indiana.edu

https://www.newscientist.com

http://tvtropes.org

https://www.theatlantic.com

http://www.cracked.com

https://tonic.vice.com

http://www.independent.co.uk

http://asexualsproject.com

http://thewip.net

http://www.openthemagazine.com